PELICAN BOOKS

A115

PREHISTORIC BRITAIN

JACQUETTA AND CHRISTOPHER HAWKES

JACQUETTA AND
CHRISTOPHER HAWKES

PREHISTORIC
BRITAIN

*

*[handwritten inscription:] Stuart P. Roberts
9, Downe Gardens
Glasgow W.*

PENGUIN BOOKS

Penguin Books Ltd, Harmondsworth, Middlesex
U. S. A.: Penguin Books Inc., 3300 Clipper Mill Road, Baltimore 11, Md
AUSTRALIA: Penguin Books Pty Ltd, 762 Whitehorse Road,
Mitcham, Victoria

—

First published 1944
Reprinted 1949, 1952
Revised edition 1958

Made and printed n Great Britain
by Hunt, Barnard & Co, Ltd, Aylesbury

Collogravure plates printed by
Harrison and Sons Ltd, London

Contents

List of Plates

A Table of Dates

THE reader will understand that the earlier these are, the less precise their accuracy becomes. Dates before about 10,000 B.C. are only rough indications; thence on to about 2000 B.C. they are (for Britain) simple approximations; thereafter, broadly speaking, they get gradually more and more accurate until exact historical dating begins with Caesar's expeditions and the Roman conquest of the 1st century A.D.

Speaking generally, the basis of the earlier dates is geological (in part also astronomical); the later ones are for the most part based ultimately upon the known chronologies of contemporary Egypt, Mesopotamia, Greece, or Rome.

	B.C.
Palaeolithic period, beginning	about 550,000
Aurignacian replaces Neanderthal Man	about 100,000
Palaeolithic period giving place to Mesolithic period	about 12,000–10,000
Maglemose culture flourishing / Britain becomes an island	about 6000
Dawn of civilization in the Near East	about 6000–5000

In Britain:

	B.C.
Neolithic period beginning	2300
Early Bronze Age: Beaker invasions	1900–1800
Early Bronze Age: Wessex invasion	1500
Middle Bronze Age: rise of Urn people beginning	1300
Late Bronze Age beginning	900
Late Bronze Age: Deverel-Rimbury invasions	750
Early Iron Age beginning	450–400
Early Iron Age: La Tène invasions beginning	250
Early Iron Age: Belgic invasions in Kent	75
Julius Caesar's expeditions	55 and 54
Early Iron Age: Belgic invasion of Commius	50

	A.D.
Cunobelin becomes king at Camulodunum (Colchester)	10
Roman conquest begins under Claudius	43

Foreword

IN a single century archaeology has pushed the beginning of human history back some half million years, and given it a perspective which was altogether lacking when knowledge was restricted to the comparatively short span of time covered by written records. And the material with which the prehistorian works is far more intimate than the documents of the historian. It is true that he lacks the romantic appeal of famous names, he cannot marshal an array of kings, heroes, and law-givers, but instead he handles the actual things which helped men to pass their lives: the pots from which they ate and drank, the weapons with which they hunted or killed one another, their houses, their hearthstones, and their graves. Such material keeps him much closer to the essentials of history. He must be concerned with the lives and achievements of countless ordinary, anonymous people.

Archaeology has enabled us to understand how, from the moment when primitive human creatures shaped the first tools, chapter after chapter has been added to the tale of man's accomplishments. He masters fire, he discovers a mechanical principle, he becomes an artist, he learns to farm, to weave, to shape pots, to sail boats, to make wheels, to cast bronze, to work iron, until imperceptibly we have reached the unfinished chapter of to-day. There is no break in this procession of events. For myself, I always see them as it were threaded on a taut line which stretches from the present near my eyes back and back into the distance of the past – a line which is in fact the historical time-sequence, the long line of the passing years. Because we are so conscious of this thread of time running through history, we have in this book held to it as a guide, following beside it for the tens of thousands of years that lead from eoliths to the Romans. A pedestrian method certainly, but one which keeps the vast complex story in good order and helps to convey the sense of continuity between the past, present, and future of humanity, which is the underlying theme.

This book wishes to be no more than the briefest chronicle of the way that he went in the small but never unimportant corner of the world that we have come to know as the British Isles.

A word on the manner of our collaboration. I have written chapters 1–4, the greater part of 5 and have added the tailpiece. My husband wrote certain parts of the fifth and the whole of the sixth chapters. More than that, his exacting scholar's eye scanned my text and allowed nothing dubious or inaccurate to pass. For this the reader will be more grateful than I was.

J. J. H.

Acknowledgements

We desire gratefully to acknowledge permission given by the following institutions, authors, and publishers for the reproduction of illustrations:

Ashmolean Museum, Oxford (pls. 8, 14, 15); British Museum (pls. 2C, 3, 5, 9, 10B, 13, 16B; figs. 9–16, 18–20); Mr M. C. Burkitt, F.S.A., and the Cambridge University Press (fig. 2); Mrs Burkitt and Prof. V. Gordon Childe, F.S.A. (fig. 3); Cambridge University Museum of Archaeology and Ethnology (pls. 2B, 16A); Dr J. G. D. Clark, F.S.A. and Messrs Methuen & Co, Ltd (fig. 19); Dr E. Cecil Curwen, F.S.A., and the same (figs. 4, 6); Mr W. J. Hemp, F.S.A. (pl. 1a); Dr P. Jacobsthal, Hon. F.S.A. (pls. 11, 12); Mr Alexander Keiller, F.S.A. (pls. 4A, 7); Central Office of Information and Ministry of Education (pl. 4B, taken by Mr Walter Bird); Oxford University Press (fig. 8); Mr C. W. Phillips, F.S.A. (pl. 2a, fig. 10); Prehistoric Society (fig. 14); Royal Commission on Ancient Monuments, Scotland (pl. 6, fig. 21); R. J. C. Atkinson and Hamish Hamilton Ltd (figs. 7a, 7b); *Illustrated London News* (pl. 10A).

Fig. 1 has been specially drawn for this book, from originals in Mr M. C. Burkitt's collection, by Mrs Burkitt, to whom we offer our particular thanks.

C. F. C. H.

Prelude

I BEGAN upon the first edition of this book in 1940, when, if one listened to the intellect alone, a German victory seemed almost certain. I was in fact preparing to write about the deepest roots of a civilization whose topmost shoots were perhaps soon to be hacked off. Seeking a justification for this fiddle-playing, I was able to suggest that although my subject was remote in time, there was yet something topical in it. There was a sudden probability that the pattern of prehistoric events would be repeated, and that the repetition would be imposed upon one's own life. As this book will show, prehistorians had spent much learning and ingenuity on reconstructing thousand-year-old stories of continental invasions of Britain. In 1940 we awaited a practical demonstration in modern form.

It was amusing to see in how many ways the present promised to mirror the past: it was even reassuring – the feeling 'this has happened before' gave perspective to one's own fate. In the early summer of the year I was living in East Anglia, where it was known that we were threatened from the Low Countries, North Germany, and Scandinavia, just the regions from which the prehistoric invaders of our Eastern coasts had usually come. Archaeological authority concurred: in early times the eastern counties were always open to invasion from just those quarters. What happened next? One by one I watched my acquaintances, openly or surreptitiously according to their natures, join a westward migration, some to south-western England, many more to Wales. Irresistibly caught up, my small son and I found ourselves in Dorset, a unit in this mass movement to the west. How reminiscent it was of an earlier Germanic onslaught, when the warlike and pagan Anglo-Saxons swept down on eastern Britain and unhappy Celts fled before them to seek safety among the western hills!

As the summer of 1940 advanced, Germanic hordes were reported to be massing down the French coast, and the whole of southern England became uneasy. This again followed the prehistoric pattern, for throughout the Stone, Bronze, and Iron Ages our southern shores had been invaded from France. In our particular western corner of Dorset we talked of the unpleasant proximity of Normandy and Brittany: of boats rumoured to be gathering at Cherbourg and Brest.

I reminded myself how Dorset had received invaders from Brittany in Neolithic times, at the beginning of the Bronze Age, and again in the Iron Age.

Then Italy. Letters from friends in Cornwall hinted that the Italians might threaten their security; others held that Ireland would be the victim. Here again prehistory could show analogies, for archaeology has proved that those areas were always accessible to movements springing from the Mediterranean, for instance, that which brought the megalithic chieftains 4000 years ago.

There could have been nothing unexpected in such repetition of the past. Whatever may be true in the future, it is clear that at that time not even aeroplanes had altered the control that geography exercises over human movements.

But now it has all grown distant and unreal, quite as far from recall as the events of prehistory; I find it hard to believe that this body of mine took part in the great exodus from Paddington, that it had a place in the trains crowded with migrating families – these things might have happened at any time. Faint and impersonal though the memory now is, this opening digression has been allowed in order to give some idea of the natural routes by which settlers and conquerors have at all times approached the British Isles. Chapter 1 will immediately follow with some account of the nature of the country itself.

The Palaeolithic and Mesolithic Ages

To all except the most urbanized among us the physical nature of our country is of profound significance. The widely differing types of scenery that Britain can offer in so small a space have entered our consciousness at an early age, beginning perhaps with the first summer holidays that took us out of a familiar scene and into a strange one. No need for knowledge of geological formations to be aware of their powerful influence on the countryside they nourish. There is an instinctive appreciation of the difference between the dry, golden feeling of the sandy heaths, the pale, clear atmosphere of the chalk, the boundless, open-skyed freedom of fenlands, and the damp chill that strikes up from the heavy clay soil of the Midlands. They appeal to different temperaments and different moods. Yet, distinctive though these several kinds of country are, they have something in common, for all belong to the lowlands of southern, central, and eastern England: an even greater contrast is to be found between these lowlands as a whole and the highlands of the west and north. Geologically the lowlands are young, and have the soft contours of youth, while the ancient rocks forming the highlands show the rugged features of a strong old age.

The line dividing these two worlds runs from east Devon to the southern boundary of Durham, but the highland zone is broken between the northern Welsh mountains and the Pennine Chain by the intrusion of the Midland Gap and the Cheshire Plain. North and west of that line one cannot be the same man that breathes south and east of it; the mountains, moorlands, swift streams, bogs, and their attendant trees, plants, birds, and fishes work a transformation. Crossing it means more than crossing the Channel, for the highland zone is far more alien to the lowland than the latter is to the adjacent parts of northern France and Flanders.

If to-day we are still acutely conscious of these divisions within our country, early man had to be much more so. Centuries of cultivation have minimized the distinctions between the various regions of the lowland zone, while modern transport hurries one without effort across boundaries that were once formidable. On Shanks' mare in a roadless land the traveller had a very different outlook. When man's ordering of the natural scene was unthought of or only just begun, he could not fail to be ever aware of the environment that was his master. What were the main geographical factors that limited prehistoric man's choice of movement and settlement? For the moment it is best to leave behind those more remote ages when Britain formed an unrecognizable part of the Continent, and deal only with the time when it had assumed approximately its present shape and temperate climate.

Consider first the forests. In prehistoric times no considerable progress was made in clearing the dense covering of oakwood and thorny undergrowth supported by the heavier and richer soils. This luxuriant growth, and the damp soil beneath, made great tracts of the lowlands, including much of the Midlands, impossible for human settlement and all but impenetrable.

In the days before drainage, marshland, too, was much more extensive; the East Anglian fens and the Vale of York formed the largest water-logged areas, but very many valley bottoms now pleasantly lined with green meadows were then swampy and hard to traverse.

It was only where soil was light and pervious, poor regions in the eyes of the modern farmer, that men were able to clear and settle the land. Hence the overwhelming concentration of prehistoric sites on chalk and limestone uplands, sandy soil, and the gravel of some valleys. For many people the great monuments of Stonehenge and Avebury, with the barrows and other satellites clustering round them, represent the essential core of all British antiquity. There is sound reason in this belief, however emotional its inspiration. The region in which they stand was all-important owing to its commanding geographical position. The physical map shows clearly how the Wiltshire Downlands form the nodal point of the lands suitable for pre-historic occupation. Not only does the chalk here reach its widest extent, but from it radiate all the principal chalk and limestone ranges of lowland Britain: the Mendips point towards the Bristol Channel; the Western Downs stretch far into Dorset; the Hampshire Downs, forking into the North and South Downs, reach the English Channel in Kent and Sussex; the Chiltern Hills linking with the East Anglian Heights penetrate to the North Sea; and finally the Cotswolds and Northampton Uplands finger northwards and make contact possible with the wide, habitable region of the Lincoln-shire and Yorkshire Wolds. Equally important, the Wiltshire Downs are accessible by navigable rivers, most significantly by the Thames, which early formed a vital thoroughfare and whose gravel-filled valley was always favourable to settle-ment. Thus the whole of this wheel-like system had a kind of unity, and on its uplands men could rear their flocks and herds, their children and their crops, looking down on the forests that pushed up between the spokes, formidable and hostile, the haunt of bears, wolves, lynx, and perhaps of evil spirits.

Very different problems confronted would-be settlers in the highland country. There the upland ranges were shunned as boggy, windswept, and generally inhospitable, the valley bottoms were blocked by oak forest, while then as now the extreme acidity of highland soil discouraged agriculture. Their choice was thus mainly limited to coastal belts such as that of eastern Scotland, where glaciers had left a more profitable soil, and to narrow coastal glens, peninsulas, and islands where well-drained ground was offered by the remains of old sea beaches. They could also take possession of the flanks of mountain valleys lying between the forested bottoms and the bleak crests above. There are signs that man could not afford entirely to ignore the high moorlands: probably he visited them during the summer when they could provide fair grazing for his beasts. Indeed, in the kinder climate of the south-west, uplands such as Dartmoor and Exmoor could be permanently settled and were at times quite populous.

Another strong contrast with the lowlands. While there we have found a general accessibility between all the habitable territories, in the mountainous country, especially in western Scotland and Wales, each little settled area tended to be cut off from the next by almost impassable barriers. To some extent, however, the prehistoric communities escaped the isolation that their land would have imposed by launching boats and finding easier and swifter passage by sea than any mountain trail could allow. Nor did their craft always hug the shore: there was often free intercourse across the Irish Sea between south-west Scotland, north Wales, the Isle of Man, and Ulster. If Ireland falls outside our main survey, she can never be forgotten. Inevitably her fate was closely linked with that of the British highlands that reached out towards her even while they walled her off from England and the Continent.

These, then, were the two great zones of Britain with their contrasting pattern of human settlement. What was the relationship between them: the reaction of one upon the other? Modern analogy has been used to show how the lowlands were always prone to invasion from the opposing continental shores, and how each wave of immigrants tended to push some of the older population into the hills. The new impulse might well itself reach the highlands, but attenuated and transfigured. Once there it would be further modified alike by a strong conservative tradition and by fresh external influences. For the highlands had their own contact with the Continent along the Atlantic sea routes from Brittany to Portugal, and thence with the Mediterranean both by sea round the coast of the Iberian Peninsula and by land across its neck. They also had an all-important asset in their possession of metal ores: gold in Ireland, tin in Cornwall, and copper in Ireland, Cornwall, north Wales, and western Scotland. Thus the highlands had distinctive ingredients to add to the British stock-pot.

The curious, intricate outline of these islands perched on the edge of Europe has from childhood become so strongly engraved on our minds that it seems to have something of unalterable truth. In fact, of course, the British Isles are very much younger than man. Human beings of a kind have inhabited our world for at least half a million years: the chalk hills that stretched across the present line of the English Channel were not finally breached until quite recently, some eight thousand years ago, while much of the North Sea was still land at an even later date.

The map of Britain began to assume its present form during the last great geological epoch, that of the Pleistocene, which covers the period often called the Ice Age. This name is misleading, for it suggests an age of continuous cold, whereas in fact it was divided into distinct cold phases, probably at least four in number, with intervals when the European climate was sometimes much warmer than at present.

At the height of the cold conditions Scotland and a great part of England lay under vast ice-sheets and glaciers; the intervening spells saw the retreat of the ice towards the north and the spread of warmth-loving plants and animals in its wake. These glaciations remodelled the face of Britain. They caused changes in sea-level, the land standing sometimes higher and sometimes lower than to-day. Thus old land surfaces could become sea floors, and the deposits then formed on them re-emerge into the air as new land, while former shorelines might be left high and dry, sometimes far inland. Melting glaciers combined with these changes in level to reshape river valleys, filling them with gravel and channelling it into stepped terraces. The ice itself exercised tremendous power. It cut and moulded the northern mountains and valleys, and farther south laid down beneath it and around its edges the accumulated material torn up and pulverized during its slow journeying. In this way was formed the boulder clay which covers so much of the Midlands; outwash from the glaciers could also spread wide expanses of plateau gravels, and far beyond the actual extent of the ice, soil formation was affected by the freezing and thawing of winter and summer. When the sheet-ice and the glaciers had finally dispersed, these deposits remained to transform the countryside, control its future vegetation, and thus ultimately do much to dictate the lines of its human settlement.

When did creatures recognizably human first begin to play their part against this geological background? It is a hard question because recognition is itself so uncertain. In the long line of ape-like figures, which shall we select as the first of our human ancestors? Perhaps it is best so to distinguish the first creature to shape a tool. For the ability to do so is exclusively human – apes may use implements but never fashion them. They were man's substitute for the specialized horns, fangs, and hoofs evolved by the beasts; although less efficient at first, they were to conquer in the end through their greater adaptability. Certainly tool-making is a more expedient criterion for the prehistorian to employ than bodily characteristics, for implements when made of stone will survive while almost all skeletal material perishes.

The idea of creating any tool artificially was entirely new – such a thing had never before happened in the world: naturally the earliest attempts would be very crude, and therefore difficult to identify. That is the position of eoliths. This name has been given to certain types of chipped flints found in Kent and East Anglia in deposits of pre-Pleistocene and early Pleistocene age. Many groups have been discredited, others may be genuine tools. But even with the most likely there is nothing to show if the chipping is artificial or merely the product of natural forces – it does not follow any of the rules of later human workmanship.

It will probably always be disputed whether these eoliths do in fact represent the first fumbling attempts of man to arm for the infinitely long struggle between Nature and himself which stretched into the future over thousands of generations. But with the scene set for the Ice Age man steps well on to the stage and begins the play in which we ourselves are acting.

The phase of human history corresponding to the Pleistocene or Ice Age of geological time is known as the Palaeolithic or Old Stone Age. It was at least a thousand times longer than the time that has elapsed since the Biblical Flood, yet the material progress achieved by Palaeolithic man was slight indeed when compared with that made by the descendants of Noah. But there was progress: slowly as he learnt more of the character of the natural resources available, he improved his equipment, shaped his tools more skilfully, and adapted them to increasingly specialized tasks. Very early, too, he learnt to make use of one of Nature's most dramatic chemical processes – fire. Behind and impelling this process of material improvement was an all-important mental growth, which was to find an outlet in coherent speech. Speech, springing from the most rudimentary beginnings, became a vehicle for carrying the fruits of experience from generation to generation. As words became more numerous, sensitive and abstract, man's intellectual conceptions could grow more complex; it is difficult for us to follow them through the medium of stones and bones, but we get a glimpse when we find him furnishing the dead with tools and food as though anticipating an after-life, and they are more fully revealed by the end of the age, when he had become master of a highly accomplished art with a magical content.

Our contacts with the earliest Palaeolithic men are confined to stone tools found incorporated in geological deposits and

Fig. 1. Flint implements of the Palaeolithic Age.

the rare discovery of actual skeletal remains; it is only later that a rather more complete and intimate picture can be drawn from the contents of cave dwellings. The earliest phases have been most successfully studied in the rich Pleistocene deposits that survive in East Anglia. These suggest that men were already shaping flints there well before the first onset of the ice, but it is not until the ensuing warmer interval that the evidence is unambiguous. But already by then two quite distinct methods of tool-making had been evolved that were to assume great importance in the future.

When confronted with the task of shaping a tool from a nodule of flint or other stone, successful results can be obtained either by chipping off the outside until the central core of the nodule emerges as the perfected implement, or by striking off a substantial flake and working that up into an implement. The core-tool will have both faces rounded and trimmed, while the other will probably have one flat face formed by the surface of the flake (Fig. 1, no. 2).

The distinction sounds slight enough, yet to primitive minds, generation after generation of which passed without thought of innovation, it would seem fundamental, and each specialized technique would be handed on unquestioningly from parent to child as an inevitable birthright.

While flake cultures are predominantly Eastern, extending right across Asia, the core cultures have an African bias: Europe, including Britain, forming the area of overlap between them. Thus from the earliest time our continent felt the benefit of a geographical position which allowed it to be enriched by two larger neighbours, Asia and Africa.

Much of Palaeolithic history is concerned with the development and interactions of these two great groups. But they must be viewed against the ebbing and flowing of the Ice Age. For when the sun was triumphant Britain became a land attractive to life of all kinds, rich vegetation clothed the countryside, elephant and rhinoceros roved from the Thames valley to

East Anglia, hippopotami floated in the rivers and wallowed in
the swamps: when the ice had the victory, southern England
alone remained habitable, and there vegetation was reduced
to a low scrub, rivers froze and valleys were blocked with
snow for many months: only such hardy animals as mammoth,
bison, and reindeer could endure even the summer weather.
And just as the big creatures replaced one another, so did the
infinitely small; everywhere among leaves and grasses, in
ponds and rivers, a host of tiny species were gradually super-
seded by others as the temperature changed, leaving their
shells to record their fate, and therewith climatic history. Man
also had to submit, almost as helplessly, for his elementary
material equipment had as yet hardly begun to give him independence of his environment. The core-culture folk at the
height of the cold phases seem, like the warmth-loving animals,
to have retreated southward towards Africa, returning again
with the milder weather. The flake peoples, on the other
hand, may have been able to survive much closer to the edge
of the ice. Each tradition shows its own cultural developments,
and these have been named after sites where they are well represented – too often for the ease of our English tongues the
chosen sites are French. The core culture which flourished
during the first interglacial phase is the Abbevillian, already
characterized by an implement always to remain the principal
core form, a heavy, pear-shaped, all-purpose tool, rather
meaninglessly known to archaeology as the hand-axe (Fig. 1,
no. 1). By the time England again became habitable this culture
had been greatly improved into the Acheulian, whose hand-
axes were more shapely, had sharper cutting edges, and owed
their smoother finish to a new method of flaking with a wooden
or bone bar in place of the hammer-stone. The Acheulian
lasted through the greater part of Palaeolithic times, the hand-
axe tending to grow lighter and more elegant and the subsid-
iary tools more varied. It should be borne in mind that our
area forms only a very small province of the Acheulian culture,

for during the immensely long life it enjoyed its bearers were able to spread all over western and southern Europe, Africa, Palestine, and much of India.

Meanwhile the flake tradition also had its innovations: every ten thousand years or so it might produce a genius with a new idea for cultural improvement or change. Contemporary with the earliest Abbevillian, apparently, there was a flake culture, which rather before the return of the Acheulians, after the second cold phase, had given rise to the Clactonian. This was a culture which in time could show excellent flint work, largely in the form of pointed and sharp-edged tools made on heavy flakes and intended for all kinds of cutting and scraping, including the dressing of animal skins. To the Clactonian and Acheulian traditions was presently added the Levalloisian; this became outstanding during the last inter-glacial, when it was responsible for beautifully finished points and scrapers which, by an ingenious new technique, were partially trimmed before the flake was struck from the parent core.

Abbevillian, Acheulian, Clactonian, Levalloisian, what do these ponderous names, based on their flinty foundations, represent in terms of human living? The economics of a very primitive food-gathering life must have demanded a small mobile group, probably united by ties of kinship (and, if we may believe Freud, already riddled with the Oedipus complex). The men would have hunted game, while the women and children gathered everything that experience had taught them was edible of fruits, roots, and grubs. Probably when the climate was warm their diet would have been predomi-nantly vegetarian: one can imagine how a week's gorging on elephant flesh might be followed by a long period when no meat was to be had. In hunting the larger animals men must have used their cunning and ability for co-operative effort to devise traps and organize drives.

As to the personal appearance of these early hunters, we

know nothing of what is usually implied by these words – hair, eyes, and complexion can be supplied only by the imagination – but we have some valuable scraps of evidence as to the bony structure which they covered. No remains likely to belong to a flake-tool maker have been found in this country, but we can turn to a contemporary who left a lower jaw to be incorporated in the Mauer sands near Heidelberg in Germany. This being must have been powerfully built and ape-like, for the jaw is chinless, but very heavy and armed with extraordinarily massive teeth. A vitally important discovery made in England allows us to form a rather more certain idea of a core-culture people. Patient watching of the quarries that are gradually biting into the mass of gravel laid down by the Pleistocene Thames had for many years yielded only animal bones and flints, but at last in 1935 part of a human skull came as a sudden reward. Its position in the Barnfield Pit at Swanscombe in association with fine hand-axes allows it to be recognized as one of the very few representatives of Acheulian man known to the world. The measurement of the two bones was followed with intense interest, which was heightened when it appeared how closely they resemble those of modern man. Other fragments came to light in 1955, but unhappily they still did not include the forehead, and so we cannot be sure whether Swanscombe Man had prominent brow ridges or a smooth brow like our own. The rest of the skull, however, is sufficiently close to *Homo sapiens* to make it reasonably certain that this man who hunted in the Thames valley some 200,000 years ago was among our own direct ancestors.

In the earlier Palaeolithic ages which we have been considering, the core and the flake traditions seem to have held aloof, each pursuing its own line of development; but in time they began to react upon each other, and in the third and last interglacial it seems that the Acheulian, Clactonian, and Levalloisian traditions actually borrowed techniques and tool-forms from one another. How far this implies also close social contacts between the two stocks is quite unknown, but it is not impossible to believe that they interbred.

One of the products of the stimulating interaction between the older traditions was a new flake culture, the Mousterian, which enjoyed its heyday during the final glaciation of the Ice Age. It is a familiar name owing to its association with Neanderthal man, that last ape-like species whose very lack of charm seems to have made him the most popular of prehistoric figures. Everyone has read of his beetling brows, his prominent teeth, his chinlessness, his hairiness, and has seen them reproduced in pictures, even in bronze busts. There is an appeal in this ape-like being who yet had the skill of a man and some of his sentiments. His tools show excellent workmanship, and he has provided the earliest known instances of the careful burial and equipping of the dead.

The last cold phase was less intense than its predecessor and was broken up by slightly milder interludes. Nevertheless living must have been harsh enough in the tundra conditions prevailing beyond the limits of the ice, and although the tough Neanderthal physique was well adapted to endure them, it is not surprising that shelter against the worst rigours of winter was sought in caves. In Britain two were certainly inhabited at this time – Kent's Cavern near Torquay, and the Pin Hole in the Derbyshire limestone ravine of Creswell Crags – the oldest recognizable human dwellings in our country.

While Neanderthal man with his Mousterian flake culture was dominant in an ice-bound continent, where were the descendants of Swanscombe man? Were any still living in western Europe? This is an unsolved problem. The Mousterian often shows borrowings from Acheulian as well as Levalloisian sources, and therefore, although none of their skeletons is known, it is not inconceivable that some descendants of the hand-axe people may have maintained themselves side by side with their more simian contemporaries. However this may be, late glacial times saw the complete triumph of our ancestral stock. With what now seems dramatic suddenness the beings whose appearance in a modern street would probably lead to their exhibition in Regent's Park were displaced by men who, if suitably clad, would hardly cause a stir at the Athenaeum, still less at the Savage. In fact, of course, this dispossession must have been spread over many generations, but it is certainly true that everywhere in Europe the Mousterian and parallel flake cultures vanish completely, together with all traces of Neanderthal Man, while his caves and hunting-grounds were taken over by men of modern type with a very different material culture. With the arrogance bred of our survival, it is very easy for us to see the Neanderthalers as low, brutish, and altogether unworthy of continuance on this earth; but if history had gone otherwise, perhaps if the weather had been rather different, how readily they would have dismissed *Homo sapiens* as a highbrow weakling fully deserving his extinction.

The late Palaeolithic hunters had a much more delicate and specialized equipment than their predecessors, that is distinguished from the core and flake forms by the general name of 'blade' culture (Fig. 1, nos. 3 and 4). Their flint implements, all much smaller and lighter than anything usual before, were often made on narrow, parallel-sided flakes and blades, which enabled them to found the tradition of the cutting knife which has remained an essential human tool ever since. In addition, these people made flint chisels which helped them to master a new technique, the carving of bone, and in time to produce beautifully finished and elaborate forms such as multi-barbed harpoons and spear-throwers in this medium. The spear-thrower has a special significance. It is the first known instance of the use of a mechanical principle, that of the lever, for supplementing mere man-power. *Homo sapiens* had already started on that career of mechanic which has him in its grip to-day.

Another important accomplishment for which the earliest evidence dates from this period is the making of fire; man had made use of it from very early times, but now he knew how to create it for himself by striking flint against a natural metallic substance, such as iron pyrites. In the bitter weather wandering hunting-parties must have been saved many hardships and dangers by their ability to light camp-fires against the cold, darkness, and beasts of the night.

These great advances in man's armament against Nature enabled him to take full advantage of the ideal hunting conditions offered in late glacial Europe, where mammoth, reindeer, woolly rhinoceros, bison, and horse throve on the steppe and tundra. In particularly favoured regions, such as south-west France and northern Spain, food supplies were now so easily obtained that the hunters had the economic security and leisure necessary to enable them for the first time to realize some of the spiritual potentialities of their humanity. Ritual, centred on hunting-magic and fertility cults, must have played a vital part in their lives, and to serve it they built up artistic schools that produced animal paintings, engravings, and carvings hardly to be surpassed in their inspired naturalism. A desire and veneration for fertility seem to have found expression in statuettes of pregnant women that often show a wonderful control of form in their full, voluptuous lines. It is one of the most astonishing events in human history that in this, its first liberation, man's artistic impulse should have created works that still, after tens of thousands of years, convey genuine aesthetic pleasure, and which can be judged without condescension by any modern standards (Fig. 2).

But these spiritual achievements were confined to the centres materially best endowed: that part of western Europe destined to become the British Isles was too remote, too ice-ridden, to support so high a standard of life. Probably the population never amounted to more than a few hundred souls, mainly absorbed in the quest for food. Caves in Derbyshire, north and south Wales, the Wye valley, and the Mendips were occupied, but the majority only sporadically and for

FIG. 2. Palaeolithic Cave paintings in France and Spain.

short periods; artistic content is extremely rare, and even flint
and bone tools are generally poor and scanty.

In France an elaborate sequence of late Palaeolithic blade
cultures has been recognized, some introduced from farther
east, some developed locally, but not all of them penetrated to
our region. The first to do so was the Aurignacian, a culture
at home between Central Europe and south-west Asia and
spreading westward finally to reach Britain as its most remote
outpost. The Aurignacians included skilled hunters and artists,
and were excellent technicians in flint, trimming their tools
with long, narrow flakes that gave an elegant fluted effect.

The next stray bands to arrive were Gravettians, a people
with a rather more northerly range than their predecessors,
who in south Russia and elsewhere had used their human wits
to prey successfully upon the formidable mammoth herds
and build up a way of life that was largely parasitic on these
great creatures. A long occupation of the Pin Hole Cave
allows us to watch the gradual evolution of the culture into a
form sufficiently distinct to warrant a name of its own, the
Creswellian. This can be saluted as the first specifically British
culture, poor cousin though it is to its brilliantly successful
French counterpart, the Magdalenian, which saw Palaeolithic
skill and artistry reach their highest perfection. A few examples
of the fine Magdalenien bone-work have been found in this
country, as far south as Kent's Cavern and as far north as the
West Riding, but we cannot guess if these were brought by
actual immigrants driven by circumstance from their own
more congenial territories, or whether, as valuable and sought-
after objects, they had been bartered from hand to hand.

The many skeletons unearthed from European caves (a
corpse in the home did not trouble and may even have encouraged these people) give a fair idea of the racial types of the
men responsible for the late Palaeolithic blade cultures. Already
they were varied, but clear correlation cannot always be established between racial and cultural divisions. There were

powerful and slight physiques, long and short faces, while round skulls existed side by side with the dominant long-head form.

Most of the late Palaeolithic inhabitants of Britain belonged to the Crô-Magnon race, tall, robust men with round but strongly boned faces, and usually, though not invariably, long-headed. Their most famous representative is the Red Lady of Paviland who was excavated in South Wales by the great Dr Buckland early in the nineteenth century. This discovery should have won prominence as the first of a Palaeolithic cave burial, but Buckland was destined to become a Dean as well as a professor of geology, and his theologian's conscience, mindful of the creation of man in 4004 B.C., obliged him to dissociate the human bones from those of the extinct animals among which they lay, and attribute them to a lady living at about the time of the Roman Conquest. His choice of names was no happier than his chronology, for the Red Lady was in fact a young man who had been ceremonially buried, together with his personal ornaments and an elephant's head, under a covering of red ochre. The use of this substance, known also on the Continent, gives a hint of the mentality of those responsible, for they may have conceived that its redness gave to ochre the life-giving power of blood.

The wealthy hunting societies of late glacial Europe might have maintained or even enriched their culture, or allowed it to stagnate and decline: they could hardly have advanced to a higher form of civilization, for the environment forbade it. But their future was not left in their own hands. Inexorably, although no doubt to them imperceptibly, the climate changed: summers grew longer and warmer, ice-sheets shrank and glaciers retreated. Enslaved to climate, plant and animal life had to change also. The mammoth, rhinoceros, and reindeer in turn disappeared from western Europe, their going perhaps accelerated by the inroads of the human hunters themselves. On what had been open grassland or tundra with a scrub of dwarf birch and willow, forests spread, stocked with the appropriate forest animals – red deer, aurochs, and wild pig. With the withdrawal or extinction of the great herds on which they had preyed, the economic basis of the hunting societies was cut away and their carefully adjusted culture made obsolete. This was one of the moments when early man was able to prove the full advantage of his self-made equipment over the biological specialization of the beasts: the reindeer found his coat intolerably hot and had to quit, man merely took his off and readjusted his habits.

The results of his labours were the Mesolithic cultures. These show two main trends in the adaptation of tool forms. One, already manifest in late Palaeolithic developments such as the Creswellian, was the reduction of the size of flints to a 'microlithic' scale, accompanied no doubt by a freer use of the now abundant wood for hafting them, several together, as composite tools. This represented little more than a compromise between the old Palaeolithic ideas and new needs. The other was the inventing of heavy wood-cutting tools to deal with that fresh factor and problem of the day, the forest. Armed with these axes, colonists were able to settle regions of northern Europe that had exchanged a covering of ice for one of trees, and there establish Forest cultures well adjusted to the changed conditions.

If these Mesolithic adaptations show no advance on Palaeolithic cultural standards, but indeed in many ways, as in the loss of art, a sad decline, they did at least allow the old human stocks to survive in Europe and conserve a physical and material contribution for the future civilization that was to reach our continent from without.

Britain received three streams of Mesolithic immigration: the Forest culture known as the Maglemosian from the east, and two of the more purely microlithic cultures, the Tardenoisian and the Azilian, from the south and south-west. They were the first to follow the three lines of approach to this country whose use, as we have seen, was to become habitual.

The newcomers must have found already in possession a poor indigenous population descended from the late Palaeolithic Creswellians. Indeed, these natives long contrived to maintain their independence, some of them migrating to Ireland thousands of years later.

The Maglemosians probably crossed the area now covered by the North Sea as fishers and fowlers, working their way over mere-studded fens, making use of dug-out canoes steered

FIG. 3. Mesolithic bone prong from the North Sea.

and propelled with broad-bladed wooden paddles. Such a canoe was found below the clays laid down by the Tay at Perth. If it is indeed Mesolithic, this is which allows Scotland to claim the oldest known boat in western Europe. On the way one of their number lost a precious bone prong from his fish-spear, which was only recovered some 10,000 years later, in 1931, when another fisherman found it in his net, trawled up from over 20 fathoms not many miles off the Norfolk coast (Fig. 3).

Once they reached the slightly higher ground that was soon to become the east coast of the British Isles, the Maglemosians occupied the river valleys and low plains suited to their means of subsistence. The men must have hunted game and small fur-bearing animals, gone fowling for duck, geese, cranes, and many other birds, and fished extensively with pronged spears, barbless bone hooks, and nets. The women's contribution of vegetable foods was augmented by the spread of trees and shrubs – hazel nuts in particular were relished – and they also would have been responsible for collecting the shell-fish that became an increasingly important element in the Mesolithic diet.

The Forest folk's great contribution to the material culture of the age, their wood-cutting tools, were at first best represented by heavy core axes, but later an improved form made on a flake, and with a wide cutting edge, largely displaced them. These tools would have been used alike for felling timber and for such carpenter's jobs as hollowing out canoes and shaping paddles.

In short, the Maglemosians enjoyed a life tolerably well provided with material comfort, at least in the summer, but they did nothing to maintain the Palaeolithic artistic traditions. Whether this was due to lack of economic plenty, and hence of leisure, or to a lack of genius, or the usual complicated balance between the two, we shall never know: perhaps it was due to fear of representational magic.

One settlement has been found in England where waterlogged and peaty mud has preserved enough of the perishable equipment of bone, antler, and wood to give a true picture of how a little Maglemosian community had lived. It is at Star Carr, near Scarborough. Here a family hunting band had established a regular camping place on the edge of one of the lakes formed by melting ice. For this was a very early Maglemose settlement established nine or ten thousand years ago, when the country was still heavily water-logged. The hunters had made themselves a convenient camping place by throwing down birch brushwood, stones, and lumps of clay on the reed-swamp bordering the lake. If they had skin tents or other shelters built on their platform, no signs of them survived. Yet they certainly worked there patiently at various crafts. First among them was making barbed spearheads by cutting strips from the shafts of red-deer antlers, and then carving them into shape. They also prepared leather and made clothes, chipped the flint tools needed for their other tasks, and, it seems, collected birch resin for attaching arrowheads to their shafts. The neat rolls of birch bark found on the platform were at first assumed to be intended for making vessels, but as no trace of such a manufacture was detected, it may be that the bark had been stripped only for the resin. The men were successful hunters of red-deer, aurochs, elk, roe-deer, and pig – these animals contributing to their diet in that order of importance, with the consumption of red-deer venison far above the rest. Oddly enough there were only a few bones of water birds and no trace of fish. It may be, however, that fish bones (like all the spear and arrow shafts) had completely decayed. In the 8th millennium B.C. northern England must still have been bitterly cold, so that in addition to clothing of furs and skins these Maglemosians had much need of fires. They evidently struck sparks with flint and iron pyrites and used a dried tree fungus for tinder.

Two finds were of outstanding interest. One, a fragment of a wooden paddle, is the oldest surviving testimony of boatmanship in the world. The other is two felled birch trees, the larger of them with a trunk 14 inches thick. The cut end is pointed, suggesting that it had been hewn by alternately driving the flint axe edge more or less straight into the trunk to make a V-shaped notch and then detaching long spalls from a foot or so higher up, until when the last fibres cracked and the tree fell the end of the trunk looked like a sharpened pencil. So here by the Yorkshire coast, we have been enabled to look for ourselves on two of the earliest of the countless trees to be felled by Stone Age man in his long-drawn struggle against the post-glacial forests.

In comparison with these Forest people the Tardenoisians are shadowy figures. Their microlithic culture originated perhaps in north Africa, whence it was obliged to expand by the increasing desiccation which there followed the end of the Ice Age. They carried it over a wide area of western Europe, probably reaching Britain from north France and Belgium. We know them almost entirely from finds of their tiny flints made on the sandy lands to which their lack of wood-cutting tools restricted them. They were also able to make summer excursions to open uplands such as the Pennines, where a number of temporary camping sites furnished with rough hearths have been preserved below the peat beds. They were a neat-fingered people, for their microliths, although often measuring no more than half an inch long, are yet meticulously trimmed – one group of them into precise geometric shapes. The majority of these pygmy flints they must have set in wooden shafts to make arrows, darts, and spears for hunting the small game and birds to their sandy territories. Dogs are now for the first time found attached to human settlements and were presumably used in the chase. The Tardenoisians can therefore claim to have originated the institution of the canine friend that has survived to become one of the most cherished and most hated of our national foibles.

The Azilians, who brought from the south of France a microlithic culture of Magdalenian descent no better adapted than the Tardenoisian to cope with forest conditions, found a different means of avoiding them in settling as strand-loopers along the coastal fringe. They were successful sea-fishermen, collected shell-fish, nuts, and probably sea-birds' eggs, went fowling, and hunted deer, boar, and smaller animals. The best known of their settlements are all in south-west Scotland, two cave shelters near Oban, and a camping site on the island of Oronsay, but others must have existed along the shores of Wales and south-west England that have since been submerged by the sea. The debt of their culture to the Magdalenian is particularly evident in their most characteristic implement, a flat, rather feebly-barbed bone harpoon which is clearly a degeneration from the elegant Palaeolithic form.

Once established in Britain, these Mesolithic cultures began to influence one another and give rise to original insular developments. One of them was that of the Horsham people who used pygmy tools like those of the Tardenoisians, but had also adopted heavy axes in the Maglemosian tradition. They it was who have left us some of the oldest artificial dwellings known in this country: a little settlement clustered round the

source of a spring at Farnham in Surrey. For shelter they had
scooped the floors of their irregularly-shaped huts well into
the ground, roofing them with boughs and perhaps with sods.

The term insular which has just been applied to these
developments of late Mesolithic times can now for the first
time be justly employed. It was almost certainly during the
Mesolithic period, and possibly about 6000 B.C. that England
became separated from the Continent. Over the fenny country
traversed by the early Maglemosians swept a rising North Sea.
It is fitting that already in the opening phase of Britain's
isolation we can watch this blending of cultures of diverse
origin and their assumption of an unmistakable local character;
it was a process often to be repeated during her future history.
For Britain now acquired the peculiar powers of an island.
Just as among the Galapagos Darwin found that island birds
evolved a special plumage, we shall see that after crossing the
Channel continental cultures assume a distinctively British
colouring. Yet she escaped the peculiar danger of an island –
stagnation through lack of stimulus. Her exposed lowlands
were always sufficiently near and hospitable to invite across the
water both colonists and traders.

Before the end of Mesolithic times changes in climate followed, and were perhaps partly caused by, these changes in
sea-level. Since the end of the Ice Age Britain had enjoyed a
climate of the 'continental' type – dry and with warm summers – but now the weather grew much wetter, south-west
winds bringing rain and mist from the Atlantic. The increasing
moisture modified the nature of the forests, driving out the
pines that had dominated them in early post-glacial days;
instead damp oak woods with abundant alder occupied all the
heavy soils, and Britain assumed the complexion described at
the beginning of this chapter, which must have lasted with no
further essential change throughout the rest of prehistoric times.

The end of an epoch was at hand. During the immense span
of time since the birth of our first tool-making human, man

had lived by taking the animals, fruits, and plants which Nature spread before him on the face of the earth. Certainly he had grown more successful, acquiring a store of knowledge and skill built up through thousands of years of bitter experience. Yet he still lived very much as the fowls of the air. He had not thought either to sow or to reap. The time for this was coming, and with it infinite possibilities for human enrichment.

Any modern visitor to Mesolithic Britain would hardly be able to guess that anything so momentous was astir. He would see poor little groups of hunters and food-gatherers scattered round the fringes and in the clearings of the dripping forests. And watching the Azilian woman crouching among the rocks as she dislodges limpets with a stone, the Tardenoisian with his flint-tipped arrow lying in wait for a hare, or even the Maglemosian leaning over the prow of his canoe with a glistening fish thrashing between the prongs of his spear, he would not think that the foundations of his civilization were being laid. Nor were they by these people, or in this country, or indeed in Europe. It was in the East that new and propitious combinations of sun, soil, water, seeds, and animal life were suggesting to men the possibility for revolutionary change.

CHAPTER 2

The Neolithic Age

THE hunting life may be a good one: dangerous, certainly, but full of excitement and free from the monotony of routine existence. Given ideal conditions it may be so easy and leisurely that it allows men time and freedom of spirit to adorn it with the joys of art and ritual. But the story already told of the catastrophic collapse of the Palaeolithic hunting civilization caused by the changing climate at the end of the Ice Age illustrates its greatest weakness: the insecurity inherent in complete dependence on natural food supplies. When the spread of forests in western Europe deprived the great herds of their livelihood, and their disappearance in turn robbed man of his, he could save himself only by the adaptability that has always been his greatest strength. We have seen how the Mesolithic cultures, with their lowered standard of living, were the best answer he could make to this challenge. But the very different problems that were posed by the contemporary changes of climate in the East provoked a totally different response. It will never be known what part individual genius and initiative played in seizing the opportunities that were offered, but the outcome is well known: man began to escape his complete subservience to his surroundings, and instead to make nature serve his own purposes.

Centres existed in the Middle East where animals and plants suitable for domestication by man flourished in conditions that prompted him to attempt it. The shifting of rainbelts across the world at the end of the Ice Age meant that while in western Europe the open grazing-grounds became wet and tree-ridden, in these more southerly zones they became, little by little, desiccated and desert. This withering of their food supply forced the animals to herd hungrily round the scattered oases, and there they would come into contact with human settlement. Thus it was natural enough that man should have the idea of exercising some control over the habits and movements of the herds that he daily saw about him. At first, no doubt, his authority was slight and his flocks lived in as nearly wild a state as the reindeer of the modern Lapp, but as the animals themselves grew more docile it increased, until with the practice of careful selective breeding man had gone far in his interference with nature.

If it was the hunting male who is likely to have been responsible for the domestication of animals, woman should probably be credited with the great parallel advance of this time – the cultivation of plants. It had always fallen to her to gather the wild vegetable foods, and when she had watched some forgotten handful of seeds sprout into new life, the notion of deliberate sowing might readily suggest itself. Here again selective propagation would in time improve the wild strains, and, granted sufficient rainfall, greatly increase their yield. We do not know which plants were the first to be cultivated, but cereals, and particularly wheat, certainly came to be the most important.

To all of us arable and pasture fields and grazing beasts are so familiar and essential a part of the countryside that it is hard to picture a world in which none such existed. Indeed, many of us go farther, and see the regular arrival of the wheaten loaf and the milk-bottle as belonging to the natural order of things. It is correspondingly difficult to think ourselves back into the lives of those who initiated the revolution that has ended in our baker's loaves and bottled milk. How would the adoption of stock-breeding and agriculture affect human living and its material progress? Obviously, while pastoralism would allow, and in some circumstances encourage, a degree of nomadism, mixed farming with agriculture would demand a much more settled way of life that was likely to lead to the establishment of village communities and an organized society. Perhaps this development affected the lives of women even more than of men: they could put down their babies in safety and have their hands and minds free to follow the practical creative bent that has always brought their greatest satisfaction. And the new type of life gave fresh scope to inventiveness. The product of their liberated genius was the many domestic crafts, such as potting, weaving, and fine basketry, which in simple societies they have continued to practise ever since.

This first great acceleration in material progress has been called the Neolithic Revolution, and it unquestionably had a deeper effect on the everyday life of men and women than any other episode in human history before the Industrial Revolution of the last centuries. And what an astounding acceleration it was! As far as we can judge, all the advances described – the invention of mixed farming and the new crafts – had been made within a few millenniums, somewhere between 7000 and 4000 B.C. – a very brief span when set against the vast, uneventful stretches of Palaeolithic time.

In the Middle East, where it began, this rapid progress was long hurried on by its own momentum. The surplus food which the new methods yielded beyond the mere subsistence of its producers not only caused a big rise in population, but made possible the support by society of increasingly skilled specialists in more and more numerous crafts. And to supply them with the needful materials a trading class was born to hunt the Near East and the Mediterranean for such rare and magical substances as malachite and obsidian and lapis lazuli, until, in time, the search was extended to metals. The discovery of the properties of copper, and then its alloy with tin, bronze, had far-reaching economic, social, and intellectual results. The ores were never obtainable in the early centres of civilization, but had to be searched out in remote mountains and carried long distances, and in response to such demands for transport came the invention of the wheeled cart and the sailing-ship. A host of new processes, many of them involving complicated chemical change, had to be devised and mastered – smelting, alloying, hammering, and casting; in fact, man was becoming a scientist, however empirical his methods.

All these activities could not be conducted from the simple villages of the old Neolithic communities; the mutual interests of the specialists drew them together and urban life began – cities grew up as centres of manufacture and commerce. Nor did the surplus wealth of the Neolithic Revolution support only artisans and traders: it also went to maintain priests and kings. By 3000 B.C. many highly organized cities were flourishing in the alluvial plains of the Tigris and Euphrates and the Nile valley. One can picture the winding streets between the mud-brick houses of the citizens – here a gem-cutter at work, there a potter spinning his wheel, weavers at their looms, a metallic tapping coming from the bronze-smith's anvil. There would be a market where country folk brought their produce – now increased by the invention of the man-driven plough to supersede the woman's hoe cultivation. And, dominating all, the great palace or temple or combination of the two, where the ruler and his satellites held power through a judicious blending of secular with magico-religious sanctions.

These vital changes in human existence were accomplished in the East while western Europe was still in the possession of the primitive Mesolithic food-gatherers described in the first chapter. But, however slowly, the results of the Neolithic Revolution could not fail to spread outward until they reached even the distant shores of Britain. Several urges combined to force this expansion of Neolithic culture. One was the increase in population which caused a perpetual demand for *lebensraum;* another was the quest for new sources of raw materials which drove ambitious prospectors and traders to explore and settle farther afield. A third and most important urge was that of the peasants, who were for ever in quest of the fresh land which their primitive agriculture was forever exhausting.

By these means new centres of Neolithic settlement grew up in the Danube basin and along the Mediterranean, where in time they, too, became urbanized and developed their own elaborate civilizations. But the farther away from its source the Revolution spread the simpler its manifestations became, until in western Europe only mixed farming and the simplest crafts were introduced. The Iberian peninsula won some importance through its mineral wealth, and here alone in the west a few settlements were large enough almost to deserve the name of cities. It was from here, from Spain and Portugal, that we shall find parties of adventurers (p. 55) setting sail for the Atlantic coasts of Britain and Ireland. But these Iberian voyagers did not form the most substantial part of the Neolithic colonizers of this country. These rather were simple farming communities which, possibly originating in pre-dynastic Egypt, had spread from the south of France northwards and westwards until groups of them began to cross the Channel to reach our southern and eastern shores. They were a slightly built people, probably often dark-haired, with long, rather narrow heads and delicate features, members of that ancient Mediterranean race that to-day can be seen at its purest among the southern Italians. We can visualize how parties of such men, women, and children pushed off in their small boats from various points along the Channel and North Sea coast, taking with them cargoes of cattle, sheep, and seed corn. Probably the Channel was still considerably narrower than to-day, and our cliffs would beckon a land-hungry people with promise of conditions similar to those they had enjoyed on the chalk of northern France. Once across the sea, the newcomers seem to have spread rapidly over the upland system (p. 15), reaching the Lincolnshire Wolds, Yorkshire, lowland Scotland and presently even across to parts of Ireland.

Now for the first time cultivated plots appeared on English

hillsides, and domestic flocks and herds grazed the uplands. Now for the first time also men banded together to construct settlements, and then tombs, on such a scale that their handiwork is still visible, the earliest marks of human activity that survive on the face of this country.

About a dozen of the distinctive entrenched settlements of the Neolithic period have been detected in southern England, from Devon to Sussex, the great majority of them on the chalk downs. The largest of them, and the most fully excavated, crowns Windmill Hill above the great temple at Avebury in Wiltshire, and, in recognition of its importance, the name of this site has been given to the culture as a whole: thus archaeologists speak, perhaps rather clumsily, of the Windmill Hill culture and Windmill Hill people. Another very interesting example lies under the racecourse on Whitehawk Hill above Brighton.

It is difficult to understand the purpose of the curious plan on which these oldest entrenchments were built. Several concentric rings of ditches and banks were dug with a considerable space between them, so that the area of the innermost enclosure may be less than a quarter of the total space encircled by the outermost ring. The ditches themselves were not continuous, but divided into short segments by solid blocks of undisturbed soil, a peculiar feature which has given these settlements the name of 'causewayed camps'. Probably, however, most of the supposed causeways had no purpose, the ditches being no more than quarries for continuous and sometimes stockaded banks; only at one or two points on the circumference would a causeway correspond with a gap in the embankment to lead (through a wooden gate) into the interior. An oval hut had stood inside the gateway at Hembury, and in several of these earthworks there were scatters of cooking pits, odd post-holes, and other marks of habitation. Often, too, fires have burned and meals been eaten in the shelter afforded by the segments of ditch. But substantial remains of settlement such as would certainly be found if these were the permanent villages of the Windmill Hill folk are lacking. Wild crab apples and hazel nuts among the rubbish suggest that the camps were generally occupied in late summer or autumn; marks of pole-axing on ox-skulls and the high proportion of the bones of young animals among the plentiful remains of cattle point to a slaughtering of livestock. Probably, then, herdsmen and their families belonging to a scattered population came up to these places in September or October (autumns would have been mild at that period) and camped out in the ditches or with only the flimsiest shelters while they branded and gelded their herds, killed off surplus stock, and dried the meat. While the men were busy with the cattle, it seems likely that the women were hard at work preparing skins from the slaughtered beasts and making them into clothes against the onset of winter.

In addition to the camps there must have been many isolated settlements dotted about the countryside, of which as yet only a few are known. On Haldon in Devon a fair-sized rectangular house with stone foundations has been uncovered, while on the hill of Carn Brea in Cornwall are the remains of round stone huts, which are probably but not certainly Neolithic. In the north of England quite a different type of dwelling existed at Ehenside Tarn in Cumberland, where a community lived in some kind of waterside settlement, paddling canoes, and perhaps catching pike with wooden tridents.

Near by the settlement we can imagine the women establishing their small gardens and corn-plots on the sunnier slopes, bending low as they tilled them with flint or stone hoes, with digging-sticks or antler picks. Their principal cereal crop was wheat, of which they grew two rather poor varieties, club wheat and emmer. When the women had gathered their modest harvest, they ground the grain in the simplest of mills, a small stone rubbed round and round by hand upon a much larger one, which in time acquired a convenient hollow top.

But of far greater importance to these people than their agriculture were the flocks and herds which the men tended and grazed on the hilltops and uncultivated slopes. Their cattle were fair-sized animals with wide-spreading horns, quite unlike the small shorthorn, *Bos longifrons*, which was to be introduced in the Bronze Age, but possibly the descendants of a cross between this breed and the great wild ox, *Bos primigenius*. The size of the herds was always limited by the wasteful necessity of slaughtering many head when grass failed in the autumn, a practice which lasted all through the Middle Ages, and could be abandoned only in the seventeenth century with the introduction of root-crops for winter feeding.

Pigs were commonly kept, and it may be supposed that they were encouraged to venture down into the forested valleys to root, and in season to fatten on acorns.

The herdsmen seem already to have used dogs to save their legs, a breed not unlike a long-legged fox terrier with small head and short back. They were evidently fed very largely on bones, for so rich were their droppings in calcium salts that they often hardened and survive for the diversion of visitors at present-day excavations.

Farm produce did not by any means entirely displace natural food supplies – men still went hunting, armed with bows and arrows tipped with fine, leaf-shaped flint heads, and brought back venison, birds, and other small game to vary the round of beef, mutton, and pork.

The domestic crafts practised by the Windmill Hill folk were simple and few – although it must never be forgotten that for every object that has survived the passage of 4000 years, scores made of perishable materials have disappeared without trace.

The women were exceptionally skilful potters, and their products make a worthy opening chapter to the long history of British ceramics. Working entirely by hand, they shaped round-bottomed bowls and jars, severely plain but usually well-proportioned and pleasing; the paste is often dark in colour, levigated with grits, and fine enough to allow quite thin walls and a well-smoothed, glossy surface (Fig. 4). They were always very sparing in their use of ornament, but occasionally would employ lines of pricks and incisions on shoulder or rim, or drag their finger-tips across the wet clay to produce a faintly fluted effect. Primitive potters are notoriously conservative, and little scope is left for individual taste – mothers would teach daughters their methods and designs, impressing upon them that theirs was the only right and proper way to make a pot, that any other would probably prove impossible and certainly unlucky. Nevertheless we do know of one Hampshire potter who, moved perhaps by a sudden whim or urge to assert herself, decorated a bowl by the imprint of a string of beads which we may imagine she took from her own neck.

FIG. 4. Neolithic pottery bowl from the flint-mines at Cissbury, Sussex.

In considering the reason for the rapid development of potting among Neolithic peoples, it is clear that with their flour pastes and other sloppy foods their need for heat-proof and water-tight vessels was much more urgent than among the Palaeolithic and Mesolithic hunters who could cook most of their foods by simple roasting on spits.

Primitive pottery forms are often derived from vessels made in other materials – baskets, gourds, and the like – and the simple baggy shapes favoured by the Windmill Hill potters may well have been copied from leather vessels; thus, though none of their products has survived, we can infer that these people were accomplished leather workers. There is no evidence for weaving earlier than the Bronze Age in this country, yet we know that it was practised by the continental kinsfolk of the Windmill Hill people, and it is hard to explain why they themselves should have lost the craft. Yet even if we find that they could make textiles, most of their clothes must have been made of leather and furs. We may be sure that many of their innumerable flint scrapers were used for cleaning and softening skins, which were then sewn with sinews threaded in bone needles.

Of Neolithic carpentry, again, very little survives, but the abundance of trees must have encouraged the use of wood. Shapely axe-hafts (Fig. 5), clubs, paddles, a trident, and the fragment of a wooden bowl from Ehenside Tarn give some slight idea of the mass of material that has perished elsewhere. No doubt also much more ambitious tasks were undertaken, such as the hollowing of boats and the dressing of timbers for house frames.

For many people the Neolithic period is rather drearily represented by the dusty rows of flints, sometimes of doubtful authenticity, which they have vaguely noticed in museum cases. Although this is an unfair conception due to the indestructibility of flint and the persistence of amateur flint collectors, there is no doubt that the output of small implements must have been very great. Simple types, such as the scrapers that bulk so largely in all these collections, could presumably have been made by every man for himself, but the very fine craftsmanship shown in some of the leaf-shaped arrowheads suggests that they were the work of specially skilled individuals. When we come to that most important part of Neo-

FIG. 5. Neolithic stone axe in its wooden haft (Ehenside Tarn Cumberland), and Early Bronze Age stone axe-hammer.

THE NEOLITHIC AGE 49

lithic accoutrement, the heavy flint or stone axes, adzes, and picks, there is no longer any question that they were made by specialists who traded them among the peasant communities. They represent, in fact, the only essential import of these communities, the one gap in their economic self-sufficiency. This specialization was necessary not only because the shaping, grinding, and polishing of such tools required much time and labour, but because their relatively large size and the need for strength demanded material that was not everywhere available.

The fine-grained stones that were particularly suitable had to be obtained from the highland zone; at Graig Lwyd in north Wales and the Langdale Pikes in Cumberland factories have been discovered where the local rock was used in such quantities that the hill-sides were strewn with the waste products of this ancient British industry. The Graig Lwyd axes were evidently of good quality, for they found purchasers as far afield as West Lothian, South Wales, Wessex, and Cambridgeshire. The Langdale products were equally popular in southern England and seem also to have been widely marketed in Scotland.

Still more remarkable was the organization required for the large-scale manufacture of flint axes, involving as it did elaborate mining operations. In order to reach the big nodules of readily workable flint that lay bedded in the chalk of southern and eastern England, pits were sunk to a depth of as much as fifty feet, often with underground galleries to follow up and exploit the richest seams (Fig. 6). The principal flint-mining centres were along the South Downs, particularly in the Worthing region, and in Norfolk at the famous site of Grime's Graves; other centres were established in Wessex. Once a good seam had been struck, shaft after shaft was sunk until several hundred might be found in a single group, often with their galleries linked together to form a vast, intricate network far below the ground. To-day such clusters show on the surface

as a confused jumble of bumps and hollows not unlike a dis-
used bombing field.

Excavation among them has given us some of the most intimate and vivid pictures of Neolithic life. We can imagine
how the miners formed a caste set somewhat apart from their
fellows, even as miners are to-day, by the mysterious and
dangerous nature of their profession, toiling unseen where
ordinary people dare not go. Laboriously they dug their pits,
working with shovels made from the shoulder-blades of
domestic animals, and with picks, hammers, and wedges of
antler, then, the flint-bed reached, drove their galleries

FIG. 6. Neolithic flint-mine (Harrow Hill, Sussex) being
cleared by modern excavators.

crouching or lying prone as they prised out the valuable nodules. The miners must have grown familiar with the maze of their subterranean burrows, but when they were long and dark they lit them with little chalk lamps: simple cups probably containing fat and floating wick. In some of the Sussex mines black patches on the roof still mark the places where these lamps burnt with a smoky flame that must have filled the galleries with strange flickering shadows, and a powerful smell.

The massive nodules, when at last they had been hoisted in baskets to the surface, were flaked into axes on the spot. Many workshops have been found, often in the shelter afforded by a partially filled shaft, where piles of flakes and wasters are proof of the mass production of a standardized tool-form.

A dramatic find made during digging at the bottom of one of the Grime's Graves pits leads on to the whole question of the magico-religious beliefs of Neolithic times. Enthroned on a ledge sat the chalk-carved image of a fat and pregnant woman, looking down on a phallus, also cut in chalk, and a great pile of deer-horn picks that had been laid as offerings at her feet. Here, in fact, was the shrine of a fertility cult, but one apparently intended to serve a curious and unexpected purpose. This particular shaft had failed to strike the usual rich flint-bed, and it seems reasonable to suppose that the shrine was set up to counteract the sterility of this pit and ensure the abundance of the next. But this was only one manifestation in the peculiar conditions of a mining community of a fertility cult that was generally practised among the Neolithic people – female figurines and phalli have been found at several causewayed camps and in a tomb, where presumably the rites were directed to more hopeful biological ends – the fecundity of men and beasts.

It is above all in tombs that we may hope to gain insight into religious belief and practice. In all Near Eastern and Mediterranean centres of civilization, and particularly in Egypt, labour and wealth were lavished on the dead to secure their contentment in the next world and hence goodwill towards their survivors in this. Equally in Britain, with their humbler resources, the Neolithic peasantry directed their greatest communal efforts to raising imposing tombs where generations of their dead could be worthily lodged.

The mausoleum that became most fashionable among the Windmill Hill people was the long barrow, an earthen mound or stone cairn built on a monumental scale that must have demanded great and well-organized labour. The stones piled into a long cairn would be at least enough to build the average parish church. Many long barrows are from 200 to 300 feet long and over 50 feet wide, and if nowadays they rarely stand more than 8 feet in height, this is in part due to the levelling processes of time.

The most familiar type of long barrow is the earthen one which has no visible architectural features. As we know them to-day (Pl. 2a), low, grassy, pear-shaped mounds lying among the lesser fry of Bronze Age round barrows, their construction looks simple enough, but when they were in commission many had structures, since collapsed, which must have given them a certain architectural quality. Such structures might include a curving façade of stout timbers across the wider end and side walls of turf or posts rising above deep flanking ditches. In some of them, too, the larger end covered some form of wooden chamber in which many bodies might be buried together.

The great majority of these earthen long barrows are to be seen along the southern chalk from Sussex to Dorset, but there are other interesting groups on the Yorkshire and Lincolnshire Wolds. A freakish example discovered below the Iron Age camp at Maiden Castle in Dorset deserves special mention, for it not only reached the fantastic length of nearly one-third of a mile, but contained a dismembered corpse that had evidently been jointed and had its skull split open to play the central rôle at a ritual feast – probably with the intention that the feasters should absorb with his flesh something of the dead man's qualities and might. But such customs cannot have been very usual among our forebears; burial in the barrows was commonly by simple inhumation, the body being crouched, perhaps to represent the natural position of sleep, or possibly to recall the foetal attitude in preparation for a rebirth after death. Sometimes, however, cremation was practised, most conspicuously in Yorkshire, where the long barrows were at times raised over specially designed trenches in which the corpses had been burnt on pyres of wood.

Another region famous for its long barrows is the Cotswold country, especially to the west, where, along the steep scarp fronting the Severn, a number are set on jutting headlands, where they can command superbly the great spreading expanse of the valley. These Cotswold barrows are not mere earthen mounds, like the majority in Sussex and Wessex; the local oolitic rock was available for the building of long cairns of neatly piled slabs, held in place with drystone walling and covering elaborate burial chambers formed with huge stone blocks or 'megaliths'. There was an essential difference in the use of this chambered type of tomb. The earthen form was a communal grave, in that it contained a number of bodies all interred simultaneously, but the stone chamber was a collective tomb intended for successive burials over a long period of time. Possibly the privilege of burial in these imposing monuments was limited to ruling families (all the skeletons in the chamber of one Wiltshire barrow showed a strong family likeness), a state of affairs that exists to-day, when the possession of a family vault is certainly an upper-class pre-rogative.

One of the best preserved and finest of these chambered long barrows is the charmingly named Hetty Pegler's Tump, near Uley, and a visit there is not soon forgotten. To enter one must stoop to pass below a massive lintel, supported on two upright blocks, into a gallery from which side cells open on either hand between towering pillars. And these few steps carry one from the familiar, brightly lit Cotswold scene into a strange cave world, with dark, shadowy entrances and a lingering ghostly presence in the air that may be felt only by the imagination but is none the less potent for that. Indeed, he would be a stone who in such an atmosphere is not tempted to materialize before him the men who once moved about in this cave of their own making, who cannot see a party of them coming through the low portal, staggering a little from the weight of the corpse which they are bearing to its sepulchre. Lifting it into one of the side-chambers, they must move aside the bones of earlier ancestors before they can deposit the body of their tribesman lying on its side with knees drawn up to chin. After celebrating the last rites and leaving with the body a few ornaments, and perhaps a bow and arrow and some pots holding food and drink, they withdraw, and carefully seal up the entrance behind them. So it will lie hidden until the day of the next funeral, but the site of the entrance remains a centre for ritual, where offerings may be laid and the ancestral spirits be propitiated or invoked.

Its ritual significance heightened the architectural importance of the portal, and when in some of the later Cotswold barrows the great central chamber was abandoned in favour of smaller cells let into the sides of the mound, the forecourt and portal were still set up, dummies leading nowhere, but providing a stage for the performance of the traditional rites.

The Cotswold barrows form only a part of a larger group of chambered long barrows centring round the Bristol Channel and the Severn. There are a number in south Wales, the best known being that called after St Nicholas, not very far from Cardiff. There are also a few eastern outliers, including the most famous of the whole group, Wayland's Smithy, that lies so beautifully on the Berkshire Downs about a mile's walk along the great Ridgeway from the equally famous White Horse of Uffington. The popularity of this grave is due more to the romantic name of Wayland than to its own inherent interest; strange that a figure so essentially of the Iron age as this legendary blacksmith, who would shoe your horse for a groat left on the roof of the smithy, should become attached to a tomb raised by a people not yet familiar even with bronze.

The Cotswold and related long barrows are not by any means the only megalithic tombs in Britain: there are hundreds, built in a variety of shapes and sizes, to be seen in the highland zone from Land's End to the Orkneys. The conspicuous manner in which they cluster along the coasts and round inland waterways with easy access from the sea suggests at once that they owed their inspiration to a maritime people who made the Atlantic and the Irish Sea their highway. Such a sea-going tradition was something so alien to the Windmill Hill peasant population that we must evidently look elsewhere for the originators of this Cyclopean architecture, and the direction to which we should turn is southwards, towards the more advanced civilizations of the Mediterranean.

The idea of building collective tombs with great stone slabs seems first to have been adopted in the western Mediterranean, where they were probably copied from similarly planned vaults hewn out of the solid rock. The mental conception underlying the idea is obscure: some have suggested that the tombs were intended as substitutes for natural caves, others that they were houses for the dead adapted from the houses of the living, others again have even ventured to recognize them as a rendering of the womb from which the spirits of the dead were to be reborn.

Whatever the explanation, it is certain that after about 2300 B.C. men were occupied in raising such monuments for their dead in Sicily, Sardinia, southern France, Spain, and Portugal. From these centres the practice was carried to the distant lands of the west and north – to Brittany and our own coasts, and then onwards to the shores of the Baltic. Soon after 2000 B.C. it must have been possible to sail the hundreds of miles from southern Spain to Sweden finding along the whole route the coasts in possession of people sharing this cultural tradition in common. But there the uniformity stopped: it is unlikely that the bulk of the megalith-building folk in the different regions would have been found to speak the same language, and they certainly did not have any common tradition for the manufacture of their tools, weapons, and pottery. For it seems that the dissemination of megaliths can be likened to that of a religion, accomplished by a comparatively small number of 'missionaries' who made converts of, and came to dominate, the local populations of many lands. We can see these elaborate tombs as everywhere merely the solid and enduring setting for a ritual cult with its own powerful magic. Visual proof of such a widespread cult is given by the curious symbolic patterns of magical significance that are carved on many megaliths in Iberia, Brittany, Ireland, and Wales, and sometimes reproduced on sepulchral pottery. Doubtless such missionaries were by no means so exclusively preoccupied with holy things as the later Celtic saints, who followed much the same routes to spread the Christian gospel and Christian architecture – their travels may have been very largely prompted by economic motives. Nevertheless they owed their success and their easy domination of native peoples to the supposed magical power that went with their control of the megalithic cult. In Britain they seem, for instance, to have had no difficulty in establishing a control of some of the Windmill Hill peasants, whose labour must have been employed for the moving and raising of the great blocks and collecting the tons of stone that went into the covering cairns.

Just as Christian churches were built to many plans at different times and among different sects – from the Orthodox basilica and the Catholic cruciform cathedral to the pseudo-romanesque Ebenezer and the tin chapel – so different groups of megalith builders believed in the virtue of their own distinctive types of tomb. Two principal plans were followed in western and northern Europe, the 'passage grave', in which a circular or rectangular chamber roofed with slabs or corbelling is approached through a narrow passage, and the 'long cist' or 'covered gallery grave', which consists simply of a long, parallel-sided burial chamber with no distinct passageway.

Both these plans are found in the British Isles, together with a host of variations from them, either in the direction of greater elaboration, or, more commonly, of degeneration due to lack of materials and labour or a decline in the zeal of the faithful.

The most ambitious and successful architects were among the followers of the passage-grave tradition whose labour and skill have given us some of the most magnificent monuments of our prehistory (Pl. 1a). Many of their greatest achievements are in Ireland, where passage-grave territory stretched to the north-west across central Ireland from the east coast, and of them all the most justly famous is the tomb of New Grange in Co. Meath. Here a huge circular cairn 280 feet in diameter and ringed with a circle of standing stones, conceals a beautifully masoned megalithic grave no less than 80 feet long, its walls and threshold (Pl. 1b) enriched with an intricate medley of magical carvings. But this is merely an outstanding example among a number of remarkable Irish graves, which are sometimes to be seen grouped together in cemeteries.

The school of megalithic art so well exemplified by the New Grange carvings can be recognized as the first important non-representational art of western Europe, and one which arose in the service of religion. Although all its motifs were derived by gradual stylization from representations of men and animals, they became at last almost entirely geometric. When reproduced incoherently as scattered patterns without any unity of composition, their purely symbolic purposes was evidently uppermost in the mind of the designer, but when, as at New Grange, there was some attempt at a general composition, the sculptor must have been genuinely concerned with the visual

effect of his work as decoration. It is an art which cannot claim
any great merit, which cannot for a moment stand comparison
with the naturalistic masterpieces of the palaeolithic hunters;
nevertheless at its best it achieved a certain effectiveness, and
merits some attention as the sole expression to have survived of
any serious decorative purpose before the growth of the beautiful secular art of the Celts more than 1,500 years later.

The men who introduced passage-grave architecture and
art seem to have reached Ireland from Portugal and south-
west Spain and to have brought with them an interest in trade
and metallurgy, including gold prospecting, which distinguished them from their more pedestrian contemporaries preoccupied with the production of food. From Ireland some sailed
for Scotland and, settling along the natural trade route offered
by the line of the Great Glen, in time established a traffic in
early copper implements – axes and halberds – then for the
first time becoming sought after in Britain. Others again,
colonized the Western Isles and more intensively the extreme
north of Scotland and the Orkneys.

Maeshowe in those islands is comparable in grandeur with
New Grange, and is so similar in construction that it must
surely have been raised for a chiefly family hailing from Ireland,
or even from Spain itself. Had the grave goods survived, they
could have given more certain information on this point, but
it so happened that some 300 years after the building of the
tomb it was robbed by a band of Vikings who chanced to
shelter there. Perhaps benighted or caught by a storm on the
moorlands, they must have made their way to the great
round artificial hill that dominated the flat landscape, and with
mingled superstitious dread and bravado have groped along
the 40 feet of passage-way to reach the spacious cruciform
chamber, where perhaps no one had set foot since the last
funerary procession withdrew some three millennia before.
One can feel gratitude to these Norsemen for whiling away
the time by cutting a runic record of their visit on the stones,

even while reviling them for the habit of plunder which prompted them to empty the grave of all trace of its original possessors.

The adherents to the rival megalithic sect of the covered gallery appear to have approached Britain from the south of France and the Pyrenees, whence their connexions may be traced even farther east in the peculiar 'Giants' Graves' of Sardinia. Sailing up the Irish Sea or round the west coast, they settled on either side of the narrows of the North Channel – in south-west Scotland, Ulster, and Man, where geographical conditions (p. 16) often dictated their splitting up into small communities, each farming a fertile valley or strip of coast. They did not strive after such ambitious architectural effects as the passage-grave people, and their tombs differ from passage graves in that they seem hardly to have been designed as buildings in which men could move freely about. Not only was the roof inclined to be low, but in many Scottish examples the cist was divided into small compartments by transverse slabs, over which it would only be possible to wriggle in a difficult and undignified manner.

As with the Cotswold chambered barrows, the covering mound was usually long in shape, and the centre of interest tended to be focused on a portal, which in the most elaborate examples was formed by two large uprights set at the centre of a semicircular façade recessed in one end of the cairn. This forecourt, a more ornate version of the splayed entrance of the Cotswold chambered barrows, must have been planned for use, and it is not too fanciful to see it filled by a circle of dancers moving in some revolving figure, while offerings might be made at the portal to propitiate the spirits of the ancestors who dwelt within.

The long-cist people did not follow the passage-grave practice of decorating their tombs with sacred patterns, but instead sometimes engraved the same designs on their sepulchral pottery. This joint possession of a common symbolism shows the underlying unity of the megalithic belief, much as the symbols of the cross and chi-ro monogram could be used to demonstrate the common Christian doctrines shared by the Catholic and Orthodox Churches. Indeed, that they were not irreconcilably torn by sectarian bigotry is shown in areas such as the Hebrides, where the passage-grave and long-cist people met and so far united as to produce a hybrid architectural tradition which presumably reflects a parallel doctrinal compromise.

There remains a small megalithic group, of which Kit's Coty House is, by reason of another attractive name, the most familiar, isolated far from the main western centres of the highland zone in the Medway valley of Kent. They had small, box-like chambers in long mounds enclosed by rectangular palings of upright stones. They may possibly have been inspired by immigrants from across the North Sea, from the Low Countries and north-west Germany, where the so-called 'Huns' Beds' are very similar in design.

The Windmill Hill peasants, with their causewayed camps and long barrows, and the megalith-building chiefs who dominated them in the west, were the sections of Neolithic society that have left us monumental survivals of their existence. But we have to consider another element in the population of the British Isles which though temporarily overshadowed by the higher cultural achievements of the invading farmers, later re-asserted itself to make a great contribution to the history of the next millennium. This was the native element, the descendants of the Mesolithic population whom the Windmill Hill folk found in possession when they arrived. While adopting some of the Neolithic innovations made available to them by the invaders, such as potting, herding, and simple husbandry, they remained generally far less settled in habit, and continued to some extent with their old mode of life as hunters and fishers. Although we have no direct evidence for it, we can reasonably assume that even in appearance they were unlike the Mediterranean type of the newcomers, for probably at least some among them had the fair northern colouring.

Obviously this native population, scattered and without strong social organization, reacted variously to the stimulus of the Neolithic way of life, so that we cannot at first expect to find among them such a compact and consistent culture as that of Windmill Hill. There are in fact a number of groups distinct yet bound together by their common inheritance from the Mesolithic past. Among these groups one of the most important was that of the Peterborough people who evidently lived in numbers along the whole length of the Thames valley and round the upper waters of the Kennet, but who also existed, probably in small roving groups, over much of eastern England. While the Windmill Hill people were attracted to the uplands, they preferred life in river valleys, by marshes and the seacoast. However, the two stocks naturally did encounter one another, particularly when after a time the Peterborough range extended farther westward. Their cultures are occasionally found mingled in Sussex and Wessex. They probably met, too, over trading ventures, for not only did the Peterborough people take some share in flint-mining, but it appears that they were the distributors, and probably also the manufacturers, of the Graig Lwyd axes from north Wales (p. 49). The adoption of distributive trading as a side-line by a hunting people is not altogether unexpected, as their few domestic ties would allow them the necessary mobility.

Very little is known of Peterborough settlements, doubtless because their houses tended to be impermanent and flimsy, and they had no conception of communal planning on the scale of a causewayed camp. The only known dwellings are round huts very much like those that sheltered their Mesolithic predecessors, with floors sunk a little into the ground and walled and roofed with small interwoven branches.

As potters the women were not highly skilled. They employed the 'coiled' method, by which long sausages of clay are laid in coils, then squeezed together and moulded with the fingers. In contrast with the Windmill Hill pottery, which at its best is so well made and unornate, the Peterborough woman favoured lavish ornament on coarse, clumsy, and often ill-fired vessels, generally round-bottomed bowls, with a thick rim and deeply hollowed neck. The ornament was produced by impressing the soft clay with twisted or whipped cord, the finger-nail, the serrated edge of a shell or the end of a small bird bone, and was scattered with more zest than discrimination over the entire surface of the pot. When, as we have seen, the Peterborough people encountered their neighbours, one of the tangible results was the adoption by the Windmill Hill potters of the idea of fairly free decoration, although they always used it with some restraint and applied it to their own superior wares.

Among Peterborough flint specialities the most interesting are arrow-heads with a broad cutting edge instead of a point, and the sickle, generally a parallel-sided blade slightly curved at the tip, specimens of which have been found with a lustre along the cutting edge that can have been produced only by friction against cornstalks.

Another form of this native Neolithic culture has been burdened with the cumbersome name of Rinyo-Clacton. Its makers lived in England in regions not very different from the Peterborough people, but one branch was established in the Orkney Islands where they had founded some very curious villages. Rinyo, on Rousay, is one of them but it is hardly so remarkable a ruin as Skara Brae on Mainland, a village that has been marvellously preserved beneath a pall of drifted sand. In the teeth of a harsh and inhospitable climate, a hardy group of colonists found it possible to form a settled community supported by herds of cows and sheep pastured on the open grassland, and by an abundant supply of shell-fish. Together these provided a staple diet which they could vary with venison, sea-birds, and fish, although no trouble was taken to devise specialized implements for hunting or fishing.

Agriculture was not practised at all. They used no metal or foreign raw materials of any kind, and were as entirely self-supporting as any Neolithic community: an independent, intimate society, often cut off from the world by gales and rough seas, and concerned with little beyond the struggle for its own existence. As in such conditions there was no need for warfare, Skara Brae economy was quite free from the burden of armaments, and if life was hard, it was peaceful. The half-dozen houses and communal workshop were huddled together for mutual warmth and shelter, the narrow alleyways between being roofed, and the whole cluster served by an efficient sewerage system of slab-lined drains.

A house consisted of a single, well-sized living-room with corbelled roof and one or more side cells that probably served as storerooms and privies. It is astonishingly good fortune to find in Britain houses largely intact after some 3500 years, but yet more fortunate that they should still contain much of their original furnishings (Pl. 6). Wood being almost un-obtainable on these windswept islands, the villagers instead used the local flagstones to build furniture that was not only convenient but imperishable. So it is that we can reconstruct complete domestic interiors and sense something of their atmosphere. And they must have been pleasant enough homes. Imagine with what relief a woman returning in the early dusk of a northern winter afternoon, perhaps with hands cold and aching after collecting shellfish, would have turned into the comparative shelter of the village alleys. Exchanging a word with a neighbour, she would duck through the low entrance of her hut until she could stand upright below her own roof and enjoy the warmth and familiar fragrance of the peat. Putting her limpets in a richly decorated pot on the stone dresser, she could sit on the edge of one of the two box-beds, with their mattresses of heather and skins, and warm her hands at the central fire. Above the bed behind her head a recess let into the wall would contain her special possessions, while opposite the store-room was readily accessible through a low doorway. Altogether nearly as well-equipped and comfortable a dwelling as many inhabited in such remote regions up to the last century. But the element of savagery was there, and one instance would not be far to seek: hidden in the foundations were the crouched bodies of two old women, buried that their spirits might hold up the walls of the house.

Skara Brae and Rinyo are a revelation of what native Neolithic herdsmen could do to meet the challenge of a difficult environment. But they must not be regarded as typical. Much more usually the Rinyo-Clacton people, like the Peterborough, would have led partly nomadic lives, often camping by rivers and lakes and coastal sand-dunes, and living in huts too humble to have left much trace behind. Yet it would be a mistake to assume that all these peoples who shared a common Mesolithic inheritance had no wider social organization than the roving family group. Evidently they must have recognized wider tribal affiliations, for they set up a number of sanctuaries, used also as burial places, that were sometimes large enough to have served a considerable community. These sacred meeting places were circular embanked enclosures, usually with the banks outside the ditches – sufficient proof that they had no defensive purpose; inside a great variety of plans were followed, some had rings or horseshoe settings of wooden posts, some had stone circles, and some no more (so far as we can tell) than a ring of ritual pits, often with cremated remains interred in or near them. The largest and probably the most important of all these Neolithic sanctuaries was at Stonehenge, but because like so many other sacred buildings of all ages it was greatly elaborated in later times it will be described when we discuss the great Bronze Age temple that was raised within it.

A remarkable example of a sanctuary with embankment and wooden settings is Woodhenge, lying not far from Stonehenge, where the bank and ditch enclosed no fewer than six concentric ovals of posts, their long axis orientated on the midsummer sunrise. Here grim evidence was forthcoming of the savage demands made by primitive religion: buried on the axis of the innermost sanctuary was the skeleton of a baby whose head had been cleft open when it was offered as a sacrifice, probably at the dedication of the temple.

Another site where the eastern type of architecture is naturally found in its purest form is at Arminghall near Norwich. This monument must in its day have been most impressive, for within its double ditch was a horseshoe setting of gigantic oak trunks, sunk 7 feet into the ground and probably rising as much as 20 feet above it.

These sanctuaries are impressive enough in themselves as examples of the religious architecture of loosely organized tribal societies. What makes them still more remarkable is that they appear to be of native British conception and are never found outside these islands. After the invasions of the Beaker folk they were to be elaborated and further foreign influences were to bring Stonehenge its unique architectural grandeur, but it now appears almost certain that the original idea behind these great circular temples must be credited to the descendants of the Mesolithic hunters and fishers of Britain.

It would be hard to over-stress the importance of the span of British history covered by this chapter. A rural economy already containing the germs of ours of to-day was suddenly imposed from without on a primitive society that had changed very little for some 20,000 years. This Neolithic settlement was, in fact, the first of the long series of contacts between Britain and the higher civilizations of the Mediterranean which have played so stimulating a part in the development of our culture. It ranks in importance beside such later influences as those of the Roman Empire, the Christian Church, and the Renaissance.

The ensuing Bronze and Iron Ages were to bring great

advances in material achievement, but nothing so fundamental as this revolution from a food-hunting to a food-producing basis for society. The growth of metallurgy and the immense improvement in equipment which it permitted, and the commercial development which it demanded, were certainly important, but it was only from soil prepared by the Neolithic economy that this growth could ever have sprung.

CHAPTER 3

The Early and Middle Bronze Ages

THE terms Stone Age, Bronze Age, and Iron Age devised more than a hundred years ago have proved of lasting value, and their very simplicity has an appeal for the ear and the imagination. Yet they should be accepted only with discretion. It must not be supposed that everywhere and all at once men abandoned their stone tools and scorned to use anything but bronze, or forgot bronze as soon as the smelting of iron had been perfected. Even to-day, with our vastly accelerated rate of material progress, we can see overlaps between an old world and a new; electricity has still failed to displace the candle from many cottages, the tractor has by no means driven the horse-drawn plough off the fields, and by going only as far afield as the Hebrides one can see corn still being ground in a stone hand-quern. In all such instances primitive forms have survived the Industrial Revolution through a combination of distance from the urban centres of civilization with poverty, often strongly reinforced by individual conservatism. These factors have always operated, and it is not surprising that in days before organized production and distribution, and before advertising, the adoption of any innovation was slow indeed. Stone tools kept a place in man's equipment through the longer part of the Bronze Age, and the majority of the stray flint implements that are hopefully assigned to the Neolithic in a host of private and some public collections were really shaped after the introduction of metal.

We have already seen how copper was in free use in the East before even Neolithic culture reached Britain, and how the first interest in metallurgy in these islands seems to have been among the passage-grave people who had settled in the Highland Zone. With copper at hand in Ireland and in lesser quantities in Scotland, and one of the most important European sources of tin easily accessible in Cornwall, the smiths of the Highland Zone were favourably placed, and they were certainly at work casting copper and bronze implements well before metallurgy was practised in lowland England.

The adoption of metal tools in England was to be accelerated by an event of outstanding importance in our prehistory: the invasion of warrior peoples from the Continent. These newcomers were not themselves great metallurgists, but they provided a ready and expanding new market for the Irish smiths, and for this reason their arrival from about 1900 B.C. is recognized as opening the British Early Bronze Age.

Archaeological whim has attached a variety of labels to the prehistoric peoples whose own names have been lost for ever: it may choose a representative site such as Windmill Hill, but sometimes a particularly characteristic item in the people's equipment is selected. Thus these first Bronze Age invaders are known as Beaker Folk, from a highly distinctive type of pot in common use among them (Pl. 3a).

Like Neanderthal Man, the Beaker Folk have been the subject of many word-portraits, in which their virility is painted with powerful adjectives. Their strong bones, muscularity, pronounced brows, and determined chins have all been emphasized, perhaps over-emphasized, while special stress has very properly been laid on the round form of their skulls, which contrasts so strongly with the neat, long heads of their Neolithic predecessors.

The previous migrations of the Beaker Folk on the Continent are among the most remarkable to have been traced by archaeology. Many believe that the cradle of the race was in inland Spain, where they were building their culture while the more advanced Megalithic people (p. 55) occupied the surrounding coasts. If this was their homeland, however, they were soon spreading vigorously through much of Europe. In central Europe and the middle Rhine they encountered and mingled with an even more warlike stock, the Battle-Axe people, who had wielded this weapon over wide territories from the Black Sea to the Baltic. In race these Battle-Axe warriors may perhaps be called 'Nordic', while it is possible that their languages belonged to that great Aryan or Indo-European family from which all the main modern European tongues descend. It was men and women in whose veins these two streams of adventurous blood were united who sailed from the Low Countries across the Channel and the North Sea to reach our coasts all the way from Sussex and Kent to northern Scotland. They came in several groups, of which the last to arrive was the most numerous and powerful, and also that in which the Battle-Axe element was strongest.

Once arrived, these several waves of energetic conquerors soon occupied the greater part of Britain, presumably dispossessing the Neolithic communities of their best pastures, and also no doubt of their herds, and sometimes of their women. Though largely ousted from the English lowlands, the Windmill Hill people survive as a physical strain in our population – that small, dark type common in the west and often mistakenly called 'Celtic' – but their culture was so thoroughly submerged that they disappeared from history, leaving only the slightest contributions to Bronze Age civilization.

The Peterborough people fared better, for with their different economy (p. 61) they had no need to compete directly with the newcomers for living space, and so survived to emerge triumphant after the force of the Beaker conquest was spent – much as the Anglo-Saxons reasserted themselves after the Norman Conquest.

But that force, while it lasted, was very great, and carried Beaker colonists and traders as far as Ireland in the west and the Orkneys in the north, although their numbers were too small to leave any very strong mark on these farthest outposts.

Granted some degree of racial unity among the beaker-users, it was an astonishing migration that seems to have taken them to central Europe and made them familiar with the Continental conditions of the Danube and the Rhine before pushing on to the most distant Atlantic shores and to islands already looking towards the Arctic. And during all this time and over all this distance they maintained their own material culture so little changed that if four sherds of beaker pottery from Spain and Bohemia, from Holland and Scotland were ranged on the palm of one's hand it might be impossible to distinguish between them.

It is not surprising to find that this restless folk, perhaps largely nomadic, were herdsmen basically dependent on their cattle, although always with a lively interest in trade. Agriculture had a place of minor importance in their economy. For dwellings tents were probably commonly used, but occasionally at least shallow circular or sub-rectangular pits were sunk into the ground and roofed perhaps with wattle, while it is likely that some of the familiar hut-circles that thrust through the Scottish and other moorland heather mark the stone foundations of Beaker dwellings.

With tools and weapons they were certainly better equipped than their predecessors, particularly in their possession of metal implements, few and simple though these were. Some of their equipment the first invaders may have brought with them from the Continent, but soon the Beaker Folk became the customers of the smiths of the Highland Zone, and particularly of the Irish smiths, from whom they purchased flat copper axes, awls, and both tanged and riveted daggers made to their own design.

This metal equipment was reinforced by implements of flint and stone. Finely chipped, tanged flint daggers were frequent substitutes for the copper and bronze forms which they imitated, and a roughly circular flint knife with the cutting edge well ground and polished was also popular. The ordinary polished axe remained in full use, while in addition the strong eastern group of Beaker Folk showed their Battle-Axe inheritance by carrying a stone axe-hammer pierced with a shaft-hole (Fig. 5, bottom), which is a simplified version of the more martial-looking continental forms.

All the Beaker people were archers, tipping their arrows with barbed flint heads and sometimes protecting their wrists from the sharp blow of the returning bow-string with stone guards: a Yorkshire warrior of wealth could afford the added elegance of gold nails to fix such a guard to its leather wristlet.

For fastening their dress they followed the prevalent Mediterranean fashion for buttons, a low, conical form being usual, sometimes carved from glossy black Yorkshire jet and embellished with a cruciform design. Jet was also used for the simple rings that acted as belt-fasteners. How much one would like to know what type of clothing such belts and buttons secured!

It seems that both linen and woollen fabrics were worn, at least by a fortunate few, for their remains have been found in graves, and it can hardly be supposed that the dead would enjoy a monopoly of these luxuries. Some few of the well-to-do also were able to deck themselves with ornaments of Irish gold, and so for the first time in Britain display that shining yellow badge that in one form or another was to remain the coveted insignia of wealth and power.

In the manufacture of the distinctive pots after which this people has been named the women showed very considerable skill, if little artistic sensibility. The paste is fine and hard, and in firing has often been allowed to oxidize to a pleasant reddish colour. Despite the really remarkable uniformity of beaker ware over its whole range, slight local variations could hardly fail to arise, and three main types were made by the different British groups. The high, expanding neck of one variety (Pl. 3a) is due to influence from the ceramic traditions of the Battle-Axe people. The ornament, usually ranged in horizontal bands and limited to a few geometric patterns of rather niggling effect, was often in finely dotted lines produced by the imprint of a toothed implement, although cord impressions and simple incisions were also employed.

Were these vessels really beakers in the sense of being primarily designed for drinking? It is very probable that they were, and it has even been suggested that they were intended for some fermented drink which helped the invaders to establish their mastery, rather as whisky has often opened the way for the less scrupulous white settlers in Africa and the Pacific, although the spiritual or magical power of alcohol may have been of greater importance.

If the Beaker Folk have left practically no domestic monuments, we are greatly indebted to them for those which they raised in the name of religion. Although never lavishing the same excessive labour on their tombs as the Neolithic communities, funerary ritual was by no means neglected. The old idea of communal burial, however, had little appeal to these roving warriors, and their dead were buried singly, crouching with the knees so close to the chin that the corpses must have been trussed into position (as in Pl. 2b). With them they laid an equipment for the next world suitable to the wealth they had owned in this: perhaps a dagger, bows, and arrows, and any ornaments that the men and women had worn during life, and in addition almost invariably they added a beaker which we can hope was left brimming with a drink potent to cheer the unknown road of death. (It is good to recollect that less than fifty years ago a Lincolnshire widow insisted on burying with him her husband's favourite beer mug.)

Very occasionally such burials might be grouped in flat cemeteries, but the traditional rite was the piling over the grave of a round mound or cairn in the shape of an inverted bowl. A number of the round barrows that are so often seen strung across the sky-lines of the chalk downs (Pl. 7), and the round cairns that dot the moorlands, were raised over our

Beaker ancestors. Sometimes the mounds cover a ring of posts that appear to represent a ritual house, occasionally they have been raised over an actual dwelling – presumably the dead man's own hut.

These barrows alone make a great contribution to the inheritance of our countryside, to the sights which in a passing moment may suddenly call the past to vivid life and fill us with a sense of ageless continuity. But still more should we thank the Beaker people for their share in the creation of two of our finest monuments: temples which as landmarks in our architectural history stand out in their period as Westminster Abbey or St Paul's in ours. Indeed, Avebury and Stonehenge are two of the most remarkable survivals from prehistoric times to be seen in western Europe. Avebury, near Marlborough, though less well known, is equally impressive: it is almost incredible that a small population furnished with humble tools of wood, bone, and stone should have the audacity to plan on such a magnificent scale. In its final form this temple comprised two pairs of concentric circles of huge stones weighing many tons apiece, standing side by side within a single stone circle, the largest of its kind in Europe, which was itself enclosed by a vast ring ditch embanked on its outer lip (Pl. 4a). The labour absorbed by this earthwork must have been immense. The chalk-cut ditch has a wide, flat bottom no less than 50 feet below the crest of the bank, and encloses an area of 28½ acres. Nor is this the whole design. Southward an avenue of pairs of stones, whose alternating tall slender and short squat shapes are thought to be male and female symbols, follows a slightly zigzag course down to the river Kennet, and thence to Overton Hill, where it terminates in another sacred enclosure known as the Sanctuary. Against the bases of two of the great stones in this avenue, and within the Sanctuary, the bodies of Beaker Folk had been buried in the usual crouched position.

The great antiquary Stukeley, who visited Avebury in the early eighteenth century, when it was much more nearly complete, records that a second avenue left the main circle to the south-west, but of this, if it ever existed, there is now little sign. Stukeley, whose early aptitude for realistic observation was overcome in later life by the growing romanticism of his century, contrived to see in the plan of Avebury the symbol of a snake, of which this south-western avenue was the tail and the Overton Sanctuary the head. Without following him into these extremes of romantic interpretation, we may legitimately allow the imagination some freedom in picturing the ceremonies for which this colossal temple was designed. We can suppose that on days of festival the uninitiated worshippers congregated on the bank to watch across the great gulf of the ditch the priests performing their mysteries on the sacred ground of the inner circles, much as a Roman audience watched gladiatorial shows from the tiered seats of an amphitheatre. What these mysteries were we shall never know; the sun certainly played some part, but did it serve only to fix the time of the festivals, or was it the actual object of their worship? There is other evidence for sun-cults in the Bronze Age, while the earth goddess and phallic fertility rites which preoccupied the mind of Neolithic man seem to have lost their hold. There was a shift of interest from the earth and the womb upwards to the sun and the heavens – well symbolized by the change from the dark, closed tomb to the open, sun-orientated temple as the principal architectural form. This change is exactly what known religious history would lead one to expect. It is typical of Indo-European religion that Zeus, a sky god, should rule the Greek pantheon. So it was the probably Indo-European element infused into our Beaker culture by the Battle-Axe warriors (p. 69) which gave its religion this skyward trend. We are witnessing the triumph of some more barbaric Zeus over the ancient Earth Mother dear to the Neolithic peasantry, the goddess whom they had brought with them from the centres of her fertile power in the Mediterranean and the Near East.

Everyone who has been to Avebury has also seen Silbury Hill. There it stands, less than a mile from the temple, in a slight circular hollow, like a steamed pudding dished up for a giant. One hundred and thirty feet high, with a base covering more than five acres, it is the largest artificial mound in western Europe. From its appearance it might well be a huge barrow built over some outstanding Early Bronze Age celebrity, but a shaft sunk from top to bottom in the eighteenth century and a tunnel driven from ground-level in the nineteenth, followed by some recent trenching, have discovered virtually nothing. Its purpose and its age remain a riddle.

Stonehenge (Pl. 4b) has always been the most visited of our prehistoric monuments; remember, for instance, the trouble and expense which Pepys endured to inspect it when on his holiday jaunt to the west country, while a host of antiquaries and artists from Tudor times onwards have left us descriptions and delightful if inaccurate engravings. Yet it can never have been so magnificent as the complete Avebury, for despite the astonishing size of its stones the whole conception was far less bold – the entire sacred area being less than one-thirteenth as great. The easiest way to recall the complexities of Stonehenge is to approach it from without. It would be following in many prehistoric footsteps to mount up to it from the river Avon along the mile-and-a-half course of the 'avenue' enclosed between its two parallel banks and ditches, for this was a road which must often have been trodden when the temple was a living centre of religion. Led by the avenue to the north-east side of the monument, one crosses the low bank and ditch by its single entrance and, walking over the ring of empty socket-holes that has been uncovered just inside the bank, passes through the great outer circle of sarsen stones and that of 'bluestones' within, to find oneself entering between the arms of a double horseshoe, the outer one formed of five colossal trilithons, the inner of small 'bluestones'. And there, across the toe of this innermost bluestone horseshoe, lies the seeming centrepiece of the whole temple, the recumbent slab of the 'altar stone' on which popular imagination has offered up many bloody victims. Standing by this altar and looking back along the axis of the horseshoes to the 'Hele Stone' at the head of the avenue, one is facing the point where the sun will rise on midsummer day.

A pitch of architectural refinement was achieved at Stonehenge unparalleled in the prehistoric west. The transverse slabs which make a continuous architrave round the outermost sarsen ring are not only curved lengthwise to fit the circumference of the circle, but grow broader towards the top to compensate for the foreshortening when viewed from the ground. In addition, they, like the cross slabs of the trilithons, are secured by mortices hollowed out to fit over tenons projecting from the tops of the uprights. All this detail becomes the more remarkable when it is remembered that enormous patience must have been required to shape such stones with no better tool than a clumsy stone maul.

The bluestones, though dwarfed by the towering sarsens about them, are in fact no less remarkable. Geology has shown that they were brought here from Pembrokeshire, whence they were probably carried most of the way by sea. This journey of at least 200 miles gives insight alike into the unexpected possibilities of prehistoric transport and the great sanctity which must already in Wales have hallowed the bluestones to prompt such a prodigious undertaking.

Because it is so extraordinary and so conspicuous Stonehenge has been the object of more speculation, and latterly of more excavation, than any other monument left to us by prehistoric man. Long recognized as the handiwork of the wizard Merlin, it was later attributed by turn to Britons, Phoenicians, Romans, Anglo-Saxons, and Danes. Even since the beginning of scientific archaeology its history has been altered very many times, and there is no reason to suppose that even the latest version will prove to be the last. Indeed, it has already been authoritatively questioned. We can hope, however, that each fresh interpretation is more nearly correct than the one before.

The results of the most recent excavations give the monument an architectural history of five or six centuries – a span of time comparable with the building and altering of many of our cathedrals. There seem to have been three principal building periods, but the last one saw several modifications. As we have seen, the place first became holy ground in late Neolithic times (p. 64) when the bank and ditch with their single entrance were made to demarcate the sacred area. This earliest Stonehenge is thought already to have included the Hele stone as a pointer and perhaps two other monoliths, now missing, at the entrance; it also saw the digging of the ring of fifty-six ritual pits inside the bank, known as the Aubrey holes. Whether these were used for the pouring of libations to gods of the underworld we are never likely to know, but certainly the Neolithic herdsmen brought the cremated remains of their dead and buried them in and near the Aubrey holes and in the silting of the ditch.

It was the construction of the second Stonehenge that can probably be attributed to the Beaker Folk. At this time, about 1700 B.C., the bluestones were brought from Pembrokeshire and set up in two closely adjoining circles, one just inside, and one just outside, the present bluestone circle. This second period also saw the making of the Avenue, almost certainly intended as a processional way. The Beaker Folk were concerned in trade with Ireland, and so might well have known the route to South Wales and have had connexions with Pembrokeshire that could explain the prodigious enterprise of transporting over eighty massive rocks from the peninsula to Salisbury Plain.

So far as we know this relatively simple sanctuary stood and remained in use for some two centuries, and through all that time seasonal festivals would have been held there at least once a year and probably much more often. Already the most important of them may have been held at midsummer, for although there was no very exact orientation in this Stonehenge of the second period, already the Hele stone and Avenue seen from the centre of the circles would have pointed in the direction of the rising sun. Then about three thousand five hundred years ago some ambitious mind resolved on reconstruction on a really colossal scale. Evidently the old temple was no longer felt to be worthy of the priests or chieftains who led the worship there. So the orders went out, and the bands of men with their thong ropes and their wooden rollers were ordered in their hundreds to the Marlborough Downs to bring back the huge blocks of sarsen. Roughly shaped before being dragged the twenty miles to the temple, they were fully dressed and the mortice and tenon joints shaped with rough stone mauls on the site itself. The activity must have been tremendous – perhaps really approaching that superhuman pitch of business always shown in reconstructions of prehistoric life. The slow hammering away at the sarsen, the tremendous concerted effort needed to erect the uprights (Fig. 7a), the slow and strenuous task of levering up the lintels (probably on wooden cribs, Fig. 7b) must have gone on for years. This third building period was complicated by various changes of plan in the use of the bluestones, now moved from their double circle. There seems to have been a plan to set them up between their present position and the outer sarsen circle but for some reason it was abandoned after the socket holes had been dug to receive them. On the other hand a few of the bluestones were carefully shaped and successfully erected in some structure that included at least two trilithons – for two of the bluestones still show pairs of mortice holes like those in the sarsen lintels, while another shows signs of having once had a tenon that must have been levelled off after the change of plan. This is at once too complicated and too doubtful a story to be told here. What is certain is that by about 1400 B.C. Stonehenge had been completed and stood in the full dignity and architectural power that we can still recognize in its noble ruin.

Who was responsible for this unique work, brilliant in concept and successful in execution? We shall see that by this period Wessex was in the hands of a very prosperous society dominated by a warrior aristocracy, who seem to have added to the riches that came to them from their herds by acting as middlemen in the trade in bronze now in full swing between Ireland and the Continent. Such powerful chiefs could well

FIG. 7a. Two stages in the erection of the uprights at Stonehenge.

have supplied the wealth (in food and men) necessary for the undertaking. But why was the architecture much more formal, its imaginative inspiration much higher, than that of any other prehistoric building in western Europe? The Wessex chiefs are known (p. 87) to have had at least trading contacts with the Mediterranean including the great maritime civilization of Minoan Crete; daggers carved on the sarsens of Stonehenge are thought by some undoubtedly to represent a type of weapon peculiar to the Mycenean civilization, the mainland Greek rival of the Minoan. The trilithons at Stonehenge can even be likened to the Postern Gate of Myceneae. A bold guess

FIG. 7b. Three stages in the raising of a lintel at Stonehenge by a crib.

has therefore been made that the British temple may have been designed by a wandering Mycenean architect working either for some Mediterranean princeling who had established himself in Wessex, or (more probably) for a native chieftain who having won a hegemony among the Wessex tribes, had the wealth and the political power necessary for the rebuilding of Stonehenge. It is a bold guess indeed, but an extraordinary explanation is called for by so extraordinary a monument.

These two great centres of worship, demanding such heavy labour and such feats of transport and engineering to build, must not be dismissed without thought of their social implications. It is clear that the acceptance of such tasks implies an immense compelling power in religion, and possibly one fostered and directed by a strong priesthood. But more than that, the ability to command such labour and the fact that the temples evidently served a considerable population and wide territories must mean some degree of social and political organization. This is the counterpart of the cultural uniformity imposed upon Britain by the Beaker conquests, and is implicit also in the far-flung commercial contacts of the conquering overlords; their ability to obtain gold, copper, and bronze from Ireland, Yorkshire jet, greenstone from Brittany. Here is the liquidation for all time of the small, self-sufficient social units of the old Neolithic era.

Stonehenge and Avebury were not, of course, the only sacred buildings of their kind, but the outstanding examples of a large class varying widely both in age and construction. We have seen that a simple kind of embanked sanctuary was already being made in late Neolithic times, the variety with a single entrance through bank and ditch like the earliest enclosure at Stonehenge. The Beaker peoples elaborated such embanked sanctuaries, preferring two entrances – or even four as at Avebury – and often setting up stone circles within them.

Such embanked monuments can be seen at Gorsey Bigbury on the Mendips, the Stripple Stones in Cornwall, Arbor Low in Derbyshire, and even as far afield as Stennis in Orkney, of these only the first is proved to have been built by the Beaker Folk, but the probability is that they had some share in the inspiration of them all, and the raising of these temples throughout Britain is further proof of the widespread religious conformity that this people was able to impose. Their orthodoxy, however, inevitably became less in regions remote from their main settlements, as is shown by their actual use of the old Megalithic collective tombs in the Scottish Isles and their adaptation of a passage-grave tradition in the remarkable 'Recumbent Stone' circles of north-east Scotland. In these the stone uprights regularly increase in size towards one side, where the tallest pair flank a massive recumbent slab, in one instance as much as 17 feet long. They were not intended to serve wholly, or perhaps even primarily, as temples, but enclosed cremated burials under a small central cairn, sometimes furnished with a passage and kerb, all reminiscent of passage-grave traditions.

Those who are familiar with the moorlands of Cornwall, Somerset, Wales, and the north of England will have seen simple circles of standing stones ranging in diameter from less than 50 to over 300 feet. Often it is not known when these were set up or by whom; some may be much later than Beaker times, but they should all fall within the limits of the Bronze Age. Perhaps the most fascinating thing about them is their names – Long Meg, the Nine, and the Merry Maidens, the Hurlers, and the Weddings, to quote a few – and the attendant folklore which tells how they are men and girls petrified for dancing and playing on the Sabbath, or wedding-parties and invading armies similarly turned to stone, and how they may return to life under the cover of darkness to dance again or drink at a nearby stream.

The tide of the Beaker invasions had swept over the whole country, inundating the Neolithic landscape, but now it began to subside and some of the old landmarks to reappear, although largely transformed as a result of their submergence. The invaders had made a great contribution to the age that was to follow, but as time went by and they became assimilated with the remains of the old population, their culture lost its narrow identity.

In northern Britain the Peterborough, Rinyo-Clacton, and other peoples of ancient Mesolithic descent emerged more vigorously, further stiffened by a strong Beaker element and with a valuable inheritance from the metallurgical and commercial interests of the passage-grave people (p. 58). The product of this mingling of races and their traditions was a distinctively British growth awkwardly named the Food-Vessel culture. The Food-Vessel province can itself be subdivided into an Irish and south-west Scottish and a north-west British region with slightly divergent lines of development.

The habits of life which had come down to them both from their Peterborough and Beaker ancestors inclined the Food-Vessel people to a nomadic existence, winning their food supplies by stock-raising and hunting, while agriculture declined yet further in importance. But commerce certainly had its place in their economy, and prompted many of them to settle along the natural trade routes of Scotland and northern England, some of which had first been opened by the passage-grave people. Here they acted as middlemen and distributors between the Irish bronze- and gold-smiths and their customers in Britain and northern Europe, while the familiar Atlantic route from Ireland carried the same goods to western France and Iberia. Ireland was becoming one of the chief mining and industrial centres of Early Bronze-Age Europe, and the Food-Vessel traders drew their share of the profits. So successful were they that they were able to deck themselves, and more especially their womenfolk, with a variety of ostentatious ornaments. How many wealthy merchants since then have used the bosoms of their wives and daughters to display before the eyes of the world bright tokens of their own success! The height of fashion for Food-Vessel women were elaborate necklets of Yorkshire jet, crescentic in shape and built up from a number of ingeniously threaded beads and engraved plaques (Fig. 8, top). Never again until Victorian ladies jangled with a host of lockets, beads, brooches, and bracelets were our native diamonds to enjoy such a vogue.

FIG. 8. Jet bead-necklace and gold 'lunula' of the Early Bronze Age.

In Ireland this necklace was rendered in a still more sumptuous medium – a sheet-gold necklet of the same crescentic shape, and chased with designs imitating the layout of the jet plaques (Fig. 8, bottom). Such necklets, known to the pedantic as *lunulae*, were exported to Denmark, north-western Germany, and France, as well as to the British market. Ear-rings of gold or bronze were also worn, of a sophisticated basket-like pattern that was perhaps originally designed by Mediterranean goldsmiths who shaped similar rings to hang in the ears of the ladies of Troy and Egypt. A little later men as well as women wore the torques made from simple gold ribbon twisted into glittering spirals.

Stone still served for many tools and weapons, of which the most individual was an oval flint knife flaked all over one surface with a skill which proves that fine flint-knapping was not yet a lost art. Bronze implements at first show little advance on those already used by the Beaker Folk, being limited to flat axes, small daggers, and halberds.

Potting was not highly accomplished. The women seem to have inherited from their Peterborough forebears an inability to fire their wares successfully, together with their rather clumsy use of the coiled technique (p. 61) and certain features from their designs – such as the hollow neck, broad decorated rim, and love of unrestrained ornament (Pl. 3b). This was particularly true in the Food-Vessel region centred in north-eastern England; in Ireland a lighter and more rounded form of bowl was usual, whose superior craftsmanship may have been due to knowledge handed down from the megalithic culture of the west.

Religious doctrine too may have drawn largely on megalithic religion, and they employed a symbolism that is only a further simplification and stylization of that shown in passage-grave art (p. 57). This is manifest also in the most famous and curious cult objects of the time, the chalk-cut idols that were found under a round barrow at Folkton in eastern Yorkshire (Fig. 9). These squat, drum-shaped idols are carved with eye symbols and owl faces that would certainly have been understood by the megalithic people of Iberia and the western Mediterranean many centuries before. Yet there is little trace of megalithic ideas in the burial customs of the Food-Vessel societies. The dead were most often buried much as the Beaker Folk had been, the bodies lying crouched under round barrows or cairns; although there might be several graves under one mound, they were essentially individual, and there is no implication of a communal rite. Another

FIG. 9. Drum-shaped chalk idol of the Early Bronze Age, from a barrow at Folkton, Yorks.

most interesting although less frequent practice was that of placing the corpse in a coffin hollowed out from an oak-trunk and sometimes shaped to resemble a boat. Here we have a reflection of the Egyptian idea of a passage by water to the next world, an idea which took firm root at this time also in Scandinavia, where it was to flower at last in the magnificent ship-burials of the Vikings. This conception would not be alien to the Food-Vessel people, many of whom must have been habitual sailors adept at driving their dug-outs far overseas on their distant trading ventures. It must have been a man with such experiences behind him who was buried under

the great cairn at Loose Howe in Yorkshire lying in a ritual
boat (similar to Fig. 10) covered by another inverted and with
a smaller one riding like a dinghy by his side.

FIG. 10. Dug-out canoes of the Bronze Age,
from the Trent at Wilford, Notts.

In addition to the food vessel itself, stone and occasionally
metal implements and ornaments, including jet necklaces,
were interred with the dead. One cannot but reflect on the
emotions of a young woman of the day when she had to watch
some coveted and perhaps irreplaceable ornament despatched
to the next world with her grandmother.

While the Food-Vessel people were left to build up their
culture and commerce in undisturbed possession of the country
north of the Thames, Wessex was the scene of more dramatic
developments. The population there was a very similar ethnic
hotch-potch of Beaker Folk and surviving Neolithic strains,
but their occupation of the heart of the chalk uplands offered
them great prosperity. They had excellent pasture for their
cattle and sheep, they had access to all quarters of England along

the uplands (p. 15), and, above all, they were well placed to handle the growing trade in metal goods, principally in bronze tools and weapons, between Ireland and Europe. The Wessex tribes seem to have been dominated by a warrior aristocracy, perhaps mainly descended from the Battle Axe element among the Beaker Folk. The Windmill Hill farmers may have contributed physically to the Wessex stock but culturally they had been overwhelmed; as in the north it seems to have been the original native element in the Neolithic population who were again in the ascendancy. With the essentials of life so easily provided, this new aristocracy was able to afford possessions far more varied and extravagant than anything known in Britain before. For their pleasure luxury goods were carried over great distances and from many quarters – the range of their trade connexions outstretched even those of the Food-Vessel people. Baltic amber was imported probably from central European *entrepôts*; bronze ornaments were also brought from central Europe, gold and bronze from Ireland, faience beads from Egypt. These gay blue beads were the first actual products of any Eastern civilization known to have reached this country, apparently through middlemen in the Aegean and Central Europe, and it is not until the days of the Roman Empire 1500 years later that we know of any others. The fact that they could be imported in considerable numbers is, then, sufficient proof of the exceptional power and organization of the Wessex chieftains. Nor was Egypt the only civilized land with which they had contacts. Many details of design and technique in Wessex ornaments and weapons show that they were influenced by the craftsmanship of Greece, where the magnificent Mycenean civilization was now at its height. The ribbed gold cup (Pl. 5a) from Rillaton in Cornwall recalls one from a rich grave at Mycenae itself, while one of the Cretan merchant princes ruling over the brilliant court of Knossos did not despise a gold-bound amber disc almost identical with pendants worn by his contemporaries in Wilt-

(a) The Chambered Tomb of Bryn Celli Ddu, Anglesey: entrance.

(b) The Chambered Tomb of New Grange, Ireland: carving at the entrance.

(a) A typical Long Barrow (Therfield Heath, Royston).

(b) An Early Bronze Age burial (Snailwell, near Newmarket).

(c) A typical Round Barrow, of the 'bell' type (Normanton, near Stonehenge).

(a) A pottery Beaker of the Early
Bronze Age.

(b) A pottery Food-vessel of the Early Bronze Age.
Diameter 7½ ins.

(a) Avebury.

(b) Stonehenge: some of the trilithons.

(a) Gold Cup of the Bronze Age, from a
grave at Rillaton, Cornwall.

(b) Pottery Cinerary Urn of the Middle
Bronze Age (Tyringham, Bucks).

Skara Brae, Orkney: a house in the Late Neolithic village (of early Bronze-Age date).

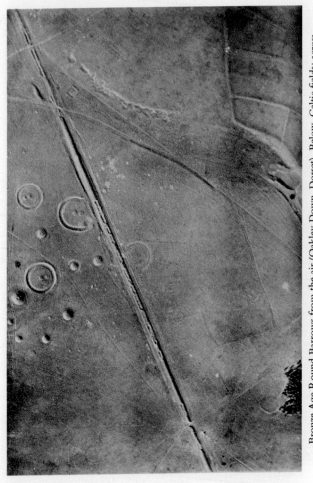

Bronze Age Round Barrows from the air (Oakley Down, Dorset). Below, Celtic fields; across the middle, a Roman road.

7

Celtic Fields on Fyfield Down, Wiltshire, from the air.

The Witham Sword. Scale, ⅔. (Of iron, with bronze scabbard-ornament).

HOPE-TAYLOR 1954

Gold cloak of the Middle Bronze Age from Mold, Flintshire.
Copyright: *Illustrated London News*.

(a) Bronze Shield of the Late Bronze Age, from
Caernarvonshire. Diameter 25 ins.

(b) Bronze figure of a boar, from Hounslow.
Length just over 2 ins.

(a) Enamelled bronze harness-mount, from Polden
Hill, Somerset. Scale, about $\frac{2}{3}$.

(b) Celtic craftsmanship in bronze: detail of an altar-top or dish from
Ireland. Scale, about $\frac{1}{2}$.

The Battersea Shield (of bronze, with red enamel in the studs). Scale, about ⅙.

Maiden Castle, Dorset: the ramparts from the air.

Uffington Castle, Berks, and the White Horse, from the air.

(a) Wrought-iron firedog, from Lord's Bridge,
Cambridgeshire, with terminals in the form of ox-heads.
Scale, about $\frac{1}{12}$.

(b) Bronze bridle-bit, from Polden Hill, Somerset.
Scale, about $\frac{1}{3}$.

shire. We have even dared to think that a Mycenean architect may have directed the final building of Stonehenge.

One of the advantages which secured the power of the new rulers was a greatly superior armament. They had daggers strengthened with a stout midrib and large enough to be formidable, and axes with flanged sides that at once increased their rigidity and allowed their hafting to be much more secure. These new forms not only outclassed the old flat daggers and axes in effectiveness, their manufacture demanded a far more advanced technique of bronze-founding that opened the way for future development. The simple, flat, open mould would no longer suffice. For these shapes with relief on two faces a double mould filled through a gate was necessary.

The Wessex chieftains also wielded heavy spherical stone maces, and used arrows tipped with exquisitely finished flint heads – long and narrow, with neatly squared, straight barbs quite unlike those of the Beaker Folk.

A fully caparisoned warrior must have made quite a splendid figure. Imagine as an example the tall, stalwart man who came to be buried under the Bush Barrow at Normanton in Wiltshire. He possessed an axe, and two massive daggers, one of which had a hilt sparkling with an intricate gold inlay and was hooked to his belt from a finely chased gold plate. Two other gold plates enriched his dress, and as a badge of rank he carried a curious sceptre with a stone head and elaborately cut bone mounts. Such sceptres suggest a truly princely pomp. Alike in meaning and in form, they are in line with their modern descendants, the ceremonial maces that so often embarrass the actors in our present-day rituals.

Even more magnificent was the ceremonial garb of a chieftain buried near Mold in Flintshire. His bones lay below their burial mound wrapped round by the largest sheet-gold object ever found in Britain. Careful reconstruction (Pl. 10) has at last proved that in his lifetime this man must have worn the gold as a short cloak fitting over the shoulders and upper arms

and dipping a little over the breast. It was secured on a bronze
framework and probably mounted on leather for greater
strength and to save chafing; as such a *pèlerine* would have
cramped the movement of the arms we can be sure that (like a
stiff shirt) it was worn only on ceremonial occasions. The
beautiful flow of the design and the rich effect of light and shade
given by the many rows of embossed ornament must have
lent the wearer a splendour altogether beyond what we have
generally imagined for our barbaric ancestors. He was probably
a contemporary of the Wessex chiefs (the cloak is dated to about
1300 B.C.) but it is unexpected to find such a mark of wealth in
north Wales.

All manner of ornaments were fashionable besides the
amber discs, faience beads, and gold plaques already described.
Beads might be made of gold, amber, or shale, and sometimes
necklaces were hung with pendants in the shape of miniature
halberds that evidently had some symbolic significance. The
women wore necklets identical with the jet crescents of their
Food-Vessel contemporaries, but made instead from a foreign
substance, amber. Amber had a strange importance in prehistoric Europe. Nor only was it decorative, but the ease with
which it became electrified gave it magical powers that had an
appeal even for the sophisticated societies of the Mediterranean.
The Baltic was almost the sole source of this precious resin,
which had lain there ever since it was exuded by the great
conifer forests of far earlier times. The trade routes that carried
it right across Europe, over the Alpine passes and down to the
Aegean, were the main channels along which ideas from the
Eastern civilizations could flow to the benighted peoples of the
north-west. Amber was a potent instrument for the diffusion
of culture. Among its largest purchasers were the Wessex
aristocrats, who imported the raw material in bulk. Not content with small ornaments, they even had it carved into
handled cups that were presumably reserved for ritual use.
Similar cups were turned from shale (and no doubt also in

wood), and to do work of this kind trained artisans must have been employed, just as bronze-smiths were needed as armourers. Among them would have been specialists in beating and engraving gold, in cutting amber, and in turning shale – living either as independent itinerants, or as camp-followers attached to the persons of the chiefs. An aristocracy, priests perhaps, a mixed peasantry, traders, miners, smiths, and other artisans: society was becoming more complex.

In their burial customs the Wessex rulers followed the round-barrow tradition first introduced into Britain by the Beaker Folk, and now widespread on the Continent. They favoured in particular two new forms of round tumulus. Among the simple 'bowl' barrows which stud the southern chalk one can often pick out a variety in which the central mound is separated by a level shelf or platform from its surrounding ditch. This is the so-called 'bell' barrow (Pl. 2c), a form of tomb which covers many of the richest chieftains' graves. In the second variety, the still more distinctive 'disc' barrow, the mound has shrunk to a mere anthill in size, ringed by a circular ditch and bank which have become the conspicuous features. Disc barrows seem invariably to mark the graves of women. Both types of monument are usually cut from the chalk with masterly precision and finish, and may be picked out in the air photograph (Pl. 7).

Bodies were still sometimes inhumed, but now for the first time cremation was the prevalent rite in southern England. The remains, whether burnt or unburnt, were contained in a wooden coffin or laid on a plank floor, and with them went the dead man's ornaments, weapons, and tools in ungrudging abundance. Specially designed funerary pottery was also used. The most interesting and charming are tiny ritual vessels, ornamented in a variety of ways, while large urns like Pl. 5b incorporate memories of beaker and other native neolithic wares.

The disc and bell barrows crowd round Stonehenge and

Avebury in numbers which prove the continued sanctity of these great temples, and we have seen that the remodelling of Stonehenge into something like its present form was apparently ordained by the lords of the Wessex culture.

The heyday of the Wessex culture, together with the Food-Vessel period of the north, is recognized as forming the second half of our Early Bronze Age. But in fact the Wessex invasion might almost equally well be said to initiate the Middle Bronze Age. Certainly one period runs imperceptibly into the next with an unbroken continuity of culture. The full Middle Bronze Age is distinguished not by anything new, but by the gradual self-assertion and expansion of the native elements in the population.

Known as the Urn people, from the large cineraries which the women made for funerary use (above), they began this expansion in about 1400 B.C., and pushed on slowly but relentlessly during the ensuing centuries of the Middle Bronze Age. At last their range was even wider than that of the Beaker Folk before them, for they not only crossed from Scotland to Ulster and effectively colonized the greater part of Ireland, but also settled regions in England such as north-east Yorkshire, Cheshire, and the Pennines, which had hitherto been shunned for the poverty of their soil. A pastoral people themselves, they had no difficulty in mingling with the Food-Vessel societies, of whom they were, moreover, close blood relations (p. 83). So it was not by force of arms, but by peaceful penetration and absorption that they succeeded in dominating their new territories. But dominate they did: gradually the Food-Vessel culture gave way before them, though not without adding to the common inheritance.

Although their main food supplies came from their flocks and the hunting of wild game, the Urn people practised agriculture, probably still simple hoe cultivation by the women-folk. They even grew a new grain, barley, side by side with the wheats that had been known since Neolithic times. Some of the earliest surviving fields to be seen in Britain were probably first tilled by them – some small, irregular plots that survive on Dartmoor and the Cleveland Hills. On Dartmoor it is easy to detect how the women, as they turned the shallow soil with their hoes, gathered into heaps or threw to the edges of their plots the stones with which they were cluttered. Their homes stood near by, on the sites now marked by 'hut circles', groups of round stone houses with clustering beehive roofs, sometimes, as at Grimspound, ringed by a protective wall. Peat smoke drifting from the roofs and through the stone-lintelled doorways would come from a central fire like those which had burned a few centuries earlier far to the north at Skara Brae.

Houses and fields have survived on Dartmoor only because the stony soil has saved it from the plough: settlements of the Urn people on more fertile lands certainly existed, but have been obliterated by long ages of cultivation. Here and there, most notably in the Thames valley, the acute eyes of air observers and their cameras have detected and recorded the ghostly outlines of ring ditches, some of which may have enclosed groups of light huts or tents. And at Rams Hill on the Berkshire Downs is a ditched counterpart of the stone-walled steadings of the moors.

As well as grain, the women raised crops of flax for linen, while the wool from their sheep they wove into materials that were sometimes of extraordinary fineness. Such fabrics were, of course, intended for clothes, and now for the first time we have a notion of prevalent fashions. No garments worn by British Urnfolk have survived, but a great deal is known of contemporary Danish costume, and dress on either side of the North Sea may well have had something in common. In Denmark oak coffins lying in waterlogged barrows have preserved for us suits of clothes complete in every detail. Men wore round woollen caps that must have been jauntily becoming, long cloaks hanging in full, graceful folds from their shoulders, and knee-length kirtles held up with woollen girdles. The women also had cloaks, but under them fashion demanded short-sleeved jackets, and skirts that could either be of woven cloth, long and formal, or a mere corded fringe just covering the knees. One lady increased the apparent abundance of her hair, which was of true Nordic fairness, by a concealed pad. The resulting bun was held in a net of intricately woven horse-hair remarkably like the nets so fashionable in Victorian days which enjoyed a revival in the 1940's.

As for ornaments to enliven such clothes, the Urn people could not generally afford the lavish display of the Wessex chiefs. Nevertheless they did contrive to secure faience beads, and some of the leading families, those who by fair means or foul owned the most head of cattle and sheep, were probably able to buy some of the wonderful gold work which is the pride of the Irish Middle Bronze Age. Most striking and opulent were the great torques made from four-flanged rods of gold twisted into glistening spirals and fastening with massive terminal hooks. These were traded not only to many parts of England, but by way of the south-western peninsula to Brittany and the Channel Isles. The most dramatic discovery was made at Grunty Fen in Cambridgeshire, when a peat-cutter, on removing a turf, saw something like a golden snake rise up from the dark soil. This was a torque which had been coiled up and buried for safety in some time of trouble well over 3000 years before.

With bronze implements the Urn people became increasingly well equipped. As the centuries passed undisturbed by foreign conquest, the British smiths used a body of skill and knowledge based on the old Irish traditions, but fertilized by the Continental ideas, to create a very successful native school of metallurgy.

Starting with the dagger and the flanged axe, they gradually adapted them to meet fresh needs. To follow the history of these technical developments archaeology resorts to one of its

favourite methods, the typological study, which in this con-
text means no more than arranging in their due order the
various stages by which the groping craftsman makes an
article more efficient, and perhaps at the same time more
beautiful, or allows it to degenerate, and perhaps to become
uglier. It is the same simple method which we all use instinc-
tively when judging by eye the date of a motor-car, a wireless
set, or a tail-coat. Many people will still be able to recollect
the evolution of the modern double-decker bus with internal
stairs from the old horse-bus with outside steps. In prehistoric
times there are few more perfect sequences of this kind than
that leading from the dagger to the socketed spear (Fig. 11).
First a long tang was added to secure the dagger blade into the
shaft of a spear; then a ferrule was found to be necessary to
prevent the shaft from splitting; next it was thought better to
make blade, ferrule, and tang in one piece; finally the central
tang was seen to be superfluous and was omitted, while loops
were added to hold thongs for binding the head to the shaft.
This process, which took place in the earlier years of the Middle
Bronze Age, ended with a thoroughly serviceable weapon
that also had a simple strength of line most agreeable to the eye.
He would be an austere functionalist indeed who could object
to the useless but pleasing pair of raised knobs on the socket
imitating the rivet-heads which in an earlier stage had served
to secure the ferrule. On the other hand when, later, the leaf-
shaped form of blade came in, the side loops were moved up the
socket into contact with its base; and when they became mere
'ornamental' openings in the wings of the blade, one should
perhaps admit degeneration. This long story of the British
socketed spear shows clearly the typological method depends
on man's natural conservatism, which prevents him from
making any abrupt break with past forms – the same unchang-
ing conservatism which to-day keeps a useless and labour-
making row of buttons on the cuffs of his coat. Without it
archaeology would often be at a loss.

The other new forms evolved at this time have less complicated histories. It is easy to see how a gradual increase in the
length of the blade accompanied by a strengthening of the
midrib would convert the dagger into the rapier of Fig. 11,
sometimes as much as 20–30 inches long, and an elegant weapon
well adapted for sticking a man in the ribs. With the axe the
problem to be solved was how best to secure it between the
forks of its haft; this was achieved by raising the height of the
flanges to prevent any up-and-down movement, and adding
a ridge across the centre to hold the ends of the fork, and so
stop the axe from pushing back and splitting its handle. In the
fully evolved palstave (Fig. 12, bottom) the problem was well
answered, although in form it was always rather uncouth,
lacking in the fine lines of spearhead and rapier. For what
purpose were these offensive weapons intended? They may
often have been used in hunting, and the axe had many practical uses, but there seems little doubt that they were primarily
intended for fighting. As the Middle Bronze Age was a period
singularly free from external dangers, one can assume that the
Urn communities fought one another, for territory and for
booty – more particularly for cattle. Even so soon do we find
man's most precious raw materials, greatest skill, and most advanced scientific knowledge dedicated to killing his own species.

Once dead, either by this means or another, the Urn people
were almost invariably cremated, the bodies being burned on
great pyres of oak logs. Their ashes were then collected in the
large cineraries after which they are named (Pl. 5b). These
great, clumsy, and often ill-fashioned jars are in a sense an enlarged variant of the Food-Vessel adapted for funerary use.
The urns were sometimes ranged in cemeteries, but much
more frequently the old round-barrow usage was continued,
the principal cremation often in a central cist with the urns of
the less distinguished dead buried round it. Occasionally the
barrow has been piled round the structure of a ritual hut in a

manner reminiscent of the earlier Beaker Folk (p. 73). For other funerals, again, the sanctuary of holy places of the past was sought, the urns being buried in the precincts of stone circles or megalithic tombs. One most remarkable site which must have been a shrine in honour of two illustrious individuals is at Bleasdale in Lancashire, where a pair of cremation urns in a central pit were surrounded by a ring of massive oak posts, a ditch with an entrance causeway, and a large outer circle of posts linked with palisading.

Doctrine concerned with an after life changed considerably in the Middle Bronze Age. The regular adoption of cremation is evidence for a less concrete conception of the fate of the physical body, a conception which is again implied by a very great simplification in the equipping of the dead. For the Urn burials are never accompanied by an elaborate display of weapons and ornaments such as went into the earth with the Wessex chiefs and the wealthier of the Beaker Folk. The gold torques, axes, spears, and rapiers are never found in graves. A poor knife, a few beads, bone pins, and belt-fasteners, occasionally a bronze razor that had probably served some ritual purpose, are the most that was left with the ashes. Evidently it was no longer considered necessary that a man should go into the next world in full pride of his earthly possessions.

This chapter has treated a stretch of British prehistory which has been conventionally and not inconveniently divided into two parts, the Early and the Middle Bronze Ages. But we have found these Ages to be so closely interlocked that the division is all but arbitrary. It is, in fact, more realistic to see the Bronze Age as opening with a time of movement, change, and diversity which passes into one of slow settling-down, assimilation, and uniformity. The first is a phase of impact on Britain from the Continent: the several invasions of the Beaker peoples, followed rapidly in the south by the growth of the Wessex culture. Then comes the calmer period after about 1400 B.C., when the various stocks old and new which had by then established themselves in the country united their blood and their traditions until, as the Urn people, they were able to spread an almost uniform culture throughout the British Isles. And this culture had time to grow insular, to develop a more distinctively British flavour than that of any previous prehistoric age. Undisturbed in these islands, the Urn communities had little concern with what went on across the sea. But, one wonders, did traders ever bring them news? Did they learn of the fall of the ancient and wealthy court of Knossos, destroyed in about 1400 B.C., probably by the Myceneans of mainland Greece? That all-important event, symbolized in Greek myth by the slaying of the Minotaur, can be said to mark the liberation of European civilization from its long dependence on the Orient. Or a generation later did they hear tell of the strange revolution led by the mystical young Egyptian pharaoh Akhenaten? How he built an entire new city where he could worship the one true god, paint, and dally with his lovely Nefertiti? That was a world far removed in spirit from the contemporary British scene, where a pastoral society was preoccupied with matters of stock-raising, hunting, and intertribal feuds. They had little in common but the memory of a few blue beads. Perhaps the Urn people would have asked nothing more than to be allowed to forget the existence of all lands beyond the Channel except for the purposes of a little quiet trade and occasional settlement. But the Continent was inexorably there, and was soon again to affect the history of Britain.

CHAPTER 4

The Late Bronze Age

THE date 1000 B.C., when (roughly) the British Late Bronze Age opens, is a good one at which to reflect on the racial pattern which was emerging on the Continent. For we are now on the edge of historic times. Soon it will begin to be possible to recognize people under their proper names. It is not always easy to remember that the very peoples whom we have met under the odd-sounding titles invented for them by archaeology, after the birth and death of a few generations will emerge into the lighted strip of history bearing such familiar titles as Celts, Germans, and Illyrians. The difficulty is to know how far back into prehistory we can legitimately push these identifications: how early, for instance, speak of Celts, when be more cautious with proto-Celts, and when the distance in time becomes too great for any name to be safely applied.

The broadest racial divisions of Europe have already been suggested in earlier chapters, and may be said to have held good from Neolithic times to the present day. These are the small, dark Mediterraneans in the south, the sturdy, round-headed Alpines along the mountain lands from the Balkans to Spain, and the tall, fair Nordics. But recognition of those subtle divisions, which are rather a question of common language and culture than of identity of blood, is much more difficult. As the Late Bronze and Iron Ages in western Europe are largely dominated by the Celts, one must ask 'Who were the Celts?' When they first began to play a part in history they are a people in process of expanding in many directions from their homelands in France and western Germany. And we know that the inhabitants of this region must have been largely descended from a mixture of Battle-Axe warriors, who were predominantly Nordic, and round-headed Beaker Folk from the south, on a solid substratum of Neolithic and ultimately Mesolithic stocks; in fact, very much the same mixture which composed the Middle Bronze Age Urn societies in Britain. We surmise that the language these Urn people spoke as they drove their flocks and hunted their game from end to end of these islands may have been already recognizably Celtic.

But the Celticization of Britain was to be continued or intensified by a series of fresh invasions during the 1000 years covered by the Late Bronze and Iron Ages. These were caused by the expansion of various Continental peoples. Away to the north of the Celtic lands Germanic tribes were breeding with their customary fecundity, while to the east of them, in Central Europe, were other virile peoples, hardly less prolific. Almost simultaneously they began the drive for more living space, the Germans crossing the Elbe and ultimately thrusting towards Holland, the Central Europeans pushing west until the effects of their pressure were felt across France as far as the Channel coasts. It was the Celtic tribes who had to absorb or give way before the impact of these western migrations. And Britain, as ever, stood open as a sanctuary for the victims of Continental upheaval.

Perhaps already before 800 B.C., a few small groups of Celts began their infiltration: some may have gone from north-west German homelands to Eastern England, while others crossed from northern France to the Kent and Sussex coasts.

One such party of refugees, probably representative of many others, established a farm in a lovely position on the South Downs, on Plumpton Plain, near Brighton. Here they made themselves a settled homestead, where they lived in round, thatched huts standing within earthen banks, linked by tracks with the cattle enclosures that lay near by. Round about the farm stretched a number of small, squarish cornfields, among the first of their kind to be tilled on British soil (p. 108). This little refugee community was evidently largely independent of the Urn people among whom it was planted, and maintained many of its Continental ways – the women, for instance, made much the same handled and incised pots which they had shaped from the clay of northern France. This was probably true of most of the colonists who reached Britain during this opening phase of the Late Bronze Age: they made little impression on the Urn communities, whose mainly pastoral and hunting life went on as before.

But already before their coming we can see the great development which distinguishes the beginning of the Late from the end of the Middle Bronze Age – a sudden adoption of many new bronze implements and a revolutionary change in the methods of the bronze industry itself. The metal was now becoming obtainable in larger and larger quantities as organization of the mining and transport of copper and tin improved. At the same time, the founders grew increasingly inventive, and devised ingenious new techniques in casting which allowed them to speed up their output and elaborate their designs. The bronze-founders present an interesting social phenomenon. They formed themselves into a wealthy class almost independent of established society, a caste of itinerants who ranged wide regions in pursuit of markets. It seems that there were no middlemen, these travelling smiths themselves making the implements they sold. They acted also as scrap-metal merchants, buying up their customers' broken or old-fashioned bronzes, probably taking them in part exchange for new types fresh from their own methods.

Travellers in little-civilized lands are always liable to meet accidents, occasionally sudden death, so it is not surprising that throughout Europe and the British Isles the contents of the bronze-smiths' workbags are found to-day in many places where they have lain since they were lost in bogs, or from capsized boats, or were buried in an emergency and never reclaimed. Such collections usually include not only finished implements, but also solid lumps of metal that have been melted down in crucibles, odds and ends of scrap, and sometimes quantities of old implements fused together into a strange, distorted mass in preparation for melting and recasting.

Merchants who traded overseas brought the Urn people new ideas for the design of implements that had been thought out on the Continent. They could offer an axe with a wide socket which avoided the weak point always present in the forked haft of the older palstave (Fig. 12, bottom). Yet the latter remained in use throughout the period, perhaps because the weight in its solid blade made it more effective for hard cutting than the light socketed form. They also brought a laurel-leaf-shaped spearhead which was pegged or tied to its haft through a pair of holes in the socket. These were efficient enough weapons, but they often suffer from a cheap, mass-produced look, and have little of the beauty of line of the native side-looped spear. A much more significant new weapon which the itinerants could put into the hands of the Urn men was a fine double-edged sword (Fig. 11), usually fitted with a leather scabbard ending in a long, tongue-shaped chape. Such swords differ from the older rapier which they displaced in being designed for slashing as well as stabbing blows. The changed manner of fighting which this design implies may well have imitated the practice of the refugees (p. 102), who would have been familiar with it in their Continental homes.

Another change for which these refugees were responsible concerns not fighting, but clothing. Whereas since Early Bronze Age times the people of Britain had generally followed the Mediterranean habit of buttoning themselves into their clothes, they now began to share the north European preference for large pins, a considerable variety of which were in fashion at this time.

Although these many new bronze forms were Continental in origin, like all foreign intrusions they soon assumed a distinctive British character. Native British craftsmen adapted the designs, and, backed by their good supplies of raw material from Cornwall and Ireland, were soon themselves exporting largely to the Continent, most freely to northern France.

In this way passed the first two centuries of our Late Bronze Age. While Greece was leaving the dark age following on the Trojan War, and was about to draw the first breath of classical civilization with the production of her austere archaic sculpture, and while Italy was cradling the strange Etruscan culture, we have seen that the pastoral Urn societies which had dominated Britain in the Middle Bronze Age continued much as before. They did little more than take full advantage of the improved equipment that was now on the market, and accept in their midst new smiths and merchants.

But in southern and south-east England their long period of undisturbed dominion was at last to be ended. The straggling immigrants of this first phase were the precursors of much more substantial Celtic invasions that began in the middle of the eighth century B.C. In the coming era the Continent was again and again to overflow on to our shores. Already in the eighth century the picture is sufficiently complicated. If some privileged being endowed with more than normal vision, exceptional patience, and a long life could have watched from a lofty peak in the centre of England, he would have had to witness wave after wave of immigrants disembarking along the east and south coasts from Yorkshire to Land's End. Straining his eyes towards the Continent for an explanation of this exodus, he could see that its prime cause was the continued land-hunger of the people there, above all the need for expansion felt among the energetic Celtic inhabitants of much of south and west Germany, parts of France, and the western Alps. He could watch their pressure westwards expelling many of the inhabitants of Holland from their old territories, until, taking to their boats, they crossed the North Sea to our eastern coast.

Meanwhile, a scrutiny of the western Alps would show him a more dramatic scene. There, securely housed on platforms rising on piles from the margins of some of the loveliest lakes in Europe, were prosperous communities not only practising sound mixed farming, but also masters of an extensive industry. They were turning out cheap bronze goods for export on a prodigious scale. Axes, spears, swords, sickles, bangles, and a host of other objects useful and decorative came pouring from their foundries. But the observer would not fail to detect that their prosperity could not endure, for a wetter climate was turning the water which had been their best protection into an immediate danger – the lakes were creeping up and threatening to flood the stilted villages. And beyond he would suddenly notice an even greater, though human, threat. Warrior tribes of south Germany had learnt from Italy and the South the use of iron, and at last, after 700 B.C., armed with powerful iron swords, they came sweeping down to complete the distress of the unhappy lake-dwellers. But already he has been watching them leave their homes and come moving towards him, their cattle, sheep, pigs, and dogs going with them. As they went, their advance had set other Celtic tribes of France in motion, and these, too, were thus now coming westward, crossing the Channel and sailing up our Wessex harbours, many of them using the excellent road into the interior afforded by the Stour-Avon estuaries at Christchurch. The French scene would show him movement from the Rhineland too, and a pressure of people from which some tribes were going northward over the narrow seas to settle in Sussex and Kent, to sail up the Thames estuary, and spread north into East Anglia. Some of those who chose the Thames estuary found that along its muddy banks it was possible to set up pile dwellings very much like those which they had left behind in the strangely different surroundings of their Alpine homelands.

Thus the second half of the Late Bronze Age was certainly a time of many invasions, but as all the immigrants were racially akin, and akin also with the native Urn folk whom they found in possession, it was easy enough for them to settle down and form a nearly uniform culture throughout the English lowlands. Much of Yorkshire and the Highland zone they never penetrated; there the Urn communities were left to follow their pastoral pursuits for several centuries longer.

These Late Bronze Age invaders have been supplied with the euphonious but cumbersome title of Deverel-Rimbury people, a double-barrel formed from two of their burial sites in Dorset. Their coming brought about a revolutionary change in the economic foundation of life in southern Britain: a very great increase in the importance of agriculture. This renewed emphasis on the raising of cereal crops was an event of deep and lasting importance in British history.

In any attempt to trace an ordered evolution in our social and economic life, periods will be encountered when there were setbacks in the main stream of development. The most familiar is that of the Dark Ages, when the growth of urban life initiated by the Romans was delayed for many centuries by the Anglo-Saxon invasions. It is true also in a much more limited sense of the Early and Middle Bronze Ages. The Windmill Hill people of the Neolithic Age belong more surely to the line of development that was to lead to the peasantry of medieval and later times than to the restless, warlike, pastoral peoples who were their immediate successors. With the coming of the Deverel-Rimbury tribes this interrupted agricultural evolution was resumed, and indeed received a sharp fillip. For they brought a new device which greatly increased the scope of cultivation. The hoe gave place to the plough, and the woman to the ox – or, more accurately, to a pair of oxen. Crop-raising was no longer to be a side-line, a small-scale tillage of garden plots, an activity that was more truly horticultural than agricultural. With the introduction of the two-ox, man-driven plough the importance of the harvest greatly increased, as corn began to be grown in regular field systems. The fields were still of modest size, in shape and area very like the small, stone-walled enclosures that are their modern descendants in Cornwall and many parts of Ireland; squarish in outline and rarely covering more than a quarter of an acre. This form of lay-out is known as the Celtic Field System, to distinguish it from the Strip System of long, narrow fields especially characteristic of Anglo-Saxon and medieval husbandry. It is not difficult to recapture an impression of our chalk country when it was covered with such little fields, for in many places their faint outlines still linger on the turf. On a ploughed slope the earth will tend to crop down towards the bottom of the field and pile up along the lower edge, until each field is separated from the one below by a slightly ridged step, while it is divided from its neighbours on either side by standing balks and the earth cast up by the turning of the plough. Banks formed in this way often show as a faint network spread on the slopes of chalk hills (Pl. 8), most clearly when picked out in shadow by a newly-risen or a setting sun.

The small size and rectangular shape of such fields was well suited to the light Mediterranean type of plough with which they were tilled, a coulterless implement which could not turn a sod, but merely scratch the surface with its short, straight share.

It would be quite false to suppose that all Deverel-Rimbury farmers were preoccupied exclusively with their crops. In many areas stock-breeding was no less important. But the old, nomadic, pastoral life was no longer suitable: communities were tied to the ploughlands in which so much labour was invested, and could no longer range freely over the open hills. Instead, pastures belonging to settled families or clans would have to be enclosed, and in many parts of the country, most conspicuously in Sussex, Hampshire, Dorset, and on Salisbury Plain, it is still possible to trace the boundaries of many such enclosures or 'ranches'. They often lay on the northern slopes of hills whose sunnier aspects were reserved for cornfields, and each was enclosed by a chalk-cut ditch 5 feet deep, with a low bank on one or both sides. The white lines of these divisions must have gleamed conspicuously across the countryside, and it is likely that they generally came to be utilized as convenient drove roads when herds had to be moved from one district to another. To-day the boundaries can often be followed for miles along the ridges, sometimes the ditch or bank showing clearly, sometimes dwindling to little more than a pale line marked by upcast chalk and flints where rabbits have burrowed more freely in the soft soil of the ditch.

In many parts of Europe early literature describes how land boundaries were first drawn with a plough, a rite whose sacred meaning was often emphasized by special ceremonies. In this manner Romulus marked the bounds of Rome. After the first ritual demarcation, the line would often, of course, be reinforced with a trench or a fence. It is therefore of special significance to notice that the form of the British enclosure ditches with their narrow bottoms and gradually splaying sides is very reminiscent of a magnified furrow. When tracing these earthworks one can believe with some confidence that their line was first trodden by a Bronze Age ploughman who, not much less than 3000 years ago, urged on his oxen to cut in the turf the first furrow of ownership. We can feel a certain pride, moreover, in knowing that they are probably the most ancient boundaries of their kind surviving in western Europe.

For the proper handling of their flocks and herds the Deverel-Rimbury people banked or ditched rectangular kraals some quarter to two acres in extent. Such places would provide shelter for lambing and calving, and perhaps in the autumn the whole clan might assemble there to help with rounding up, slaughtering of surplus stock, and the salting of meat for the winter larder.

For their more permanent homes many of them owned

small steadings very like those built by the first Late Bronze Age settlers on Plumpton Plain (p. 102). Not many miles west of this older farm a Deverel-Rimbury family established itself on the summit of New Barn Down above Worthing. There a hollowed track led one along the down between the neat array of small fields, then, turning sharply across the ridge, entered a rectangular farmyard, protected on one side by a bank and ditch and on the others by a fence set on a low bank. Inside the enclosure rose the conical, thatched roofs of some half-dozen circular huts and barns, ranged round a small, open yard. It was a compact, well-planned little farm, where life could be ordered and secure, one of many scattered over the uplands of southern England.

A very different type of dwelling was chosen by a wealthy Late Bronze Age group in the north of England. Possibly the choice was not a free one, but forced upon them to escape some danger, otherwise it is difficult to understand why such people should want to live in a narrow, dark, and excessively damp cave overlooking the little Heathery Burn, near Stanhope in County Durham. They occupied it long enough to break a great amount of crockery and to eat a great amount of beef, mutton, and game, throwing the fragments and the bones cheerfully on the floor. Their equipment was astonishingly rich, including quantities of socketed axes, spears, swords, tools, and ornaments and even a mould and tongs for the practice of bronze founding. An elegant shouldered bucket of Irish type (Fig. 13, 2) and a golden armlet and ring must have been even more strangely out of place in these dank and wild surroundings. So many and excellent were their possessions that one cannot fail to wonder if the cave were the temporary home of an exiled chief and his followers. This idea gains colour from the fact that the group certainly included a bronze-smith and probably brought with them a four-wheeled horse-drawn cart, both of which are likely to have been the prerogatives of a man of rank. If one may be permitted a momentary flight of fancy, one can see the party fleeing after some defeat, possibly at the hands of the first Iron Age invaders (p. 118), the leader accompanied by his retainers and his smith, forcing their

FIG. 13. Bronze cauldron and bucket of the
Late Bronze Age (from Ireland)

way into these remote regions, horses struggling to drag the fine cart over rough, difficult country. And it is likely that their tenancy of the cave had an even more violent conclusion. Why were so many valuables abandoned on the floor, and why were the bones of at least three human beings found among them? It seems that some catastrophe, probably a sudden spate in the ravine, must have caught them unawares, thus ending in tragedy a story which we believe began in misfortune.

Still farther to the north a little Bronze Age settlement was established at Jarlshof in the Shetlands, where a few stone-built houses sheltered among the dunes close by Sumburgh Head. The villagers lived simply but efficiently, making the best use of whatever was to hand in a country so cold and exposed as those islands. They kept herds of shorthorn cattle and two breeds of sheep, cultivated their fields, and also hunted seals and went fowling and fishing. Their solidly built houses were of a curious plan, perhaps first devised in the Mediterranean and then introduced here by the Megalithic folk. From a central courtyard with a hearth opened four little side-chambers contained in the thickness of the wall, while opposite the entrance was a large alcove which could serve as a cattle stall. One ingenious householder tethered his cattle to a stall-ring fashioned from a whale's vertebra, and appears also to have collected cowdung for his fields – the first recorded instance of the use of manure by a British farmer.

At first the community was as nearly self-sufficing as their Early Bronze Age predecessors at Skara Brae, fashioning their implements from bone and the local slate and quartz, and even carving domestic pots out of soft rocks. But towards the end of the Late Bronze Age an event occurred which must have caused great excitement among the simple villagers and served to link them with the outside world. A bronze-smith suddenly arrived in the hamlet, set up his workshop in one of the courtyards, and began to mould swords, knives, pins, and other articles that must have impressed the locals as representing the height of luxury and scientific wonder. We can suppose that the smith, on the contrary, felt himself wretchedly benighted, and often cursed an unjust fate which had deprived him of his more comfortable livelihood farther south. For he may well have been one of the victims of the blacksmiths and their new metal, whose arrival in Britain threatened many of the bronze-founders with unemployment (p. 118).

If Late Bronze Age domestic arrangements show some improvements in the social amenities, the varied abundance of goods obtainable by the end of the period must have meant a much greater advance in the standard of living – and of killing. To consider the latter art first. The new offensive weapons, the sword, spear, and axe already described, as they came to be produced more cheaply and in larger quantities, must have reached an ever-widening section of the population. At the same time defensive armament was reinforced. Warriors could now protect themselves with round shields, either wooden with a bronze boss over the handgrip, or all of bronze, the sur-face often enlivened by ring within ring of little *repoussé* knobs (Pl. 11a).

Those invaders of south-east England who came from the Alpine lakes brought their own distinctive bronze types; their swords had parallel sides instead of bulging blades, and ended in a long, tapering, sinister-looking point, while their axes were a peculiar winged elaboration of the old flanged form (Fig. 11).

But improvement was not restricted to weapons of war: men and women were also infinitely better equipped for their peaceful callings. Specialized tools were ready to the hand of the craftsman: socketed gouges and chisels for the carpenter, hammers, tracers, punches, tongs, and miniature anvils for the bronze- and gold-smiths. To reap his increasing corn crops, the field worker could use a well-designed socketed sickle, while for the wealthy housewife cooking facilities were vastly improved by the introduction of sheet-bronze cauldrons (Fig. 13, top). In these great, fat, round-bellied vessels, fitted with ring handles for hanging them over the flames, food could

be seethed and stewed in an appetizing manner hitherto impossible. Their design was copied by the Irish smiths from the
Mediterranean, where such cauldrons are already often mentioned in Homeric verse. From Ireland they were imported
as luxuries into Britain, a fact recalled by the tale in the Mabi-
nogion that tells how a certain British king was the proud
owner of one which had been brought over to him by an
Irishman, 'a huge, reddish-yellow-haired man, coming up
from the lake with a cauldron on his back'. Everywhere their
possession was recognized as a certain mark of rank and
wealth.

A second type of bronze vessel then in fashion, the high-
shouldered bucket, far more elegant and formal in taste than
the portly cauldron, was of a Central European design that
came to be widely imitated in western Europe (Fig. 13, bottom).

Other domestic crafts to advance their methods in the Late
Bronze Age were spinning and weaving. For the first time
there is evidence that spindles for twisting the yarn were
weighted with round 'whorls' to increase their spin, while some
form of upright loom was adopted in which the warp threads
were held taut by cylindrical clay weights.

Improved weaving must have led to better clothes, and with
them many ornaments were worn. Gold was still freely imported from Ireland. In contrast with this wealth of goods for
the living, the dead were more poorly provided than at any
other time in our prehistory, and there is an almost complete
absence of new religious monuments of any kind. This need
not mean that the Deverel-Rimbury people were stern ration-
alists, that a wave of agnosticism swept Britain in the Late
Bronze Age; their religious tenets may even have been more
spiritual and less superstitious than those held at other times,
but certainly their beliefs did not impel them to great labours
in the building of temples or tombs, or to great sacrifices for
the enrichment of their dead. They had inherited from central
Europe the custom of cremation burial in large cemeteries or

'urnfields'. The true central European urnfield had no grave-mounds, but in the west the old Battle-Axe warrior tradition was still sufficiently alive for low saucer-shaped barrows often to be raised over the cremations, or for the urns to be buried in the flanks of older tumuli. In Britain this persistence of the barrow idea was particularly strong in Wessex. No durable possessions went with the ashes into these cineraries, and the urns themselves, even at their most ornate, can show no more than plain lugs, flutings, or bands of clay corrugated with the impressions of the potter's fingertips. Indeed, of all the dreary sights to be seen in our museums, none is more inevitably dreary than the contents of an average large Deverel-Rimbury cemetery: row upon row of barrel-shaped or cylindrical urns, dark in paste, often lop-sided and ill-fired. Yet their very number, so wearying to the eye, has a special importance. It signifies the very great growth in population which better agriculture made possible by increasing food supplies, until by the end of the Late Bronze Age southern England was more thickly settled than ever before.

After 1300 years the British Bronze Age was reaching its close. While in the north many of the old Urn Folk were still semi-nomadic pastoralists, the south was rich in settled hamlets and steadings surrounded by their arable fields and grazing grounds. Cheap bronze had made good tools and weapons available to many, and the merchants who supplied them grew in wealth and importance. There was better farming and crafts-manship, better clothes, more food and better cooking. Al-together a sufficiently prosperous land. Nor was the coming of the new age of iron to make any profound change in its structure. The bronze workers were naturally the hardest hit. These proud inheritors of a craft which in Britain had well over a millennium of tradition behind it had either to adapt them-selves or succumb. In the Lowland Zone iron was gradually to displace bronze for the manufacture of tools and weapons, so that the founders were faced with the choice of learning to

work iron, casting only the ornaments and fittings that continued to be made in the more beautiful old metal, or retreating
to trade on a humbler scale in the Highland Zone, where
bronze long held its own. We have already encountered one
such impoverished merchant driven to seek his living at
Jarlshof.

It was not that iron was at first greatly superior to bronze –
indeed, it was little harder and in appearance far more uncouth
– but it was plentiful. Much of the bronze-smiths' power had
depended on their knowledge and control of the sources of
two raw materials: copper, which was far from common,
and tin, which was even rarer. But with iron there was no need
for such elaborate organization – ores could be found in abundance and in many places. Once its smelting was understood,
once furnaces could be brought to a sufficient heat, iron could
be produced far more cheaply and readily than bronze. Its
adoption in Britain, therefore, really only intensified a social
process already begun in the Late Bronze Age – the putting of
good tools and weapons within the reach of the many instead of
the few.

Iron had been used by man very long before it was first
brought to Britain. In Mesopotamia and Egypt it was occasionally used as early as 3000–2500 B.C. But it was the Hittites
of Asia Minor who first began to work it on a large commercial
scale, trading it freely among their neighbours in the eastern
Mediterranean, and it was from them that the craft first reached
Europe, where it became known to the Greeks by the end of the
second millennium B.C. The warriors with iron swords whom
we have seen driving out the Alpine Lake-dwellers after about
700 B.C. (p. 106) were sharers in the first widespread European
iron-using civilization, that of Hallstatt, which originated in
central Europe, but soon spread among the Celtic tribes of the
west. At about this time the worsening of the climate which
had flooded the lake villages began to have a serious effect on
the farming communities of northern Europe. Threatened with

famine, many were obliged to migrate southward, and it was mainly this cause, combined with a universal growth in population due to the development of agriculture, which sent further groups of Celts across the Channel, bearers of a late version of the Hallstatt culture. So it was that the first true British Iron Age began in southern England in the fifth century B.C.

The Early Iron Age

ALTHOUGH the use of iron was not general in Britain before the immigrations that began in the fifth century B.C., the vigorous Hallstatt civilization of central Europe, with its groups of restless swordsmen, did not fail to make itself felt at an earlier date. Already by the sixth century adventurers with knowledge of Hallstatt ways were percolating into these islands armed with swords that were usually made of bronze, yet followed the design of the iron weapon. Such pioneering groups exerted some influence on the Late Bronze population, and in particular we find the native bronze-smiths casting modified versions of their Hallstatt swords.

Some of them even arrived possessed of iron implements, and taught the smiths how to forge iron. One among them whom we may treat as representative of the rest was a warrior who seems to have sailed from western France to establish himself in south Wales on the fertile land of the Glamorgan Plain. Native hillsmen in the Black Mountains, envious of his property, organized a sally down to the Plain and looted his household. But as they were retreating triumphantly back towards their own fastnesses some alarm made them throw their booty into the mountain lake Llyn Fawr, where it was to lie for some two thousand five hundred years. The prize had been a rich one. It included two of the precious bronze cauldrons, which bobbed some little way across the surface of the lake before becoming water-logged and sinking. Then there were spearheads and axes of ordinary Late Bronze types, but the chief had also owned a Hallstatt bronze razor and a sickle made of iron. The sickle had evidently been wrought by a native craftsman faithful to his traditional bronze patterns, however ill-suited to the new metal. Most remarkable of all was a great iron sword which, though native in some of its details, in form and size and in the curious winged shape which adorned its scabbard closely resembled the weapon carried by the Hallstatt swordsmen of the Continent (Fig. 11).

Settlers of this kind who used iron implements, and had the blacksmiths to forge them, acted as heralds of the true Iron Age which began in the fifth century B.C., when changes of climate and land shortage drove large numbers of fresh invaders to our shores. These came in several groups, landing all round our eastern and southern coasts, just as their precursors had done in the Late Bronze Age. The eastern seaboard received colonists from the Low Countries, among whom Hallstatt civilization was already much diluted, so far had they lived from its greatest centres. For this reason they were readily able to fuse with a British Bronze Age population with which they had much in common, and so build up a culture in which old traditions mingled with new. It was otherwise in Wessex, where Celts from northern France imposed a more advanced Hallstatt culture which took comparatively little from that of the old Deverel-Rimbury people.

If in much of the south of Britain this transition from the last Bronze Age to the first Iron Age was clear-cut, while in the east it was blurred, in neither did it very greatly change the habits of life developed during the previous centuries. The backbone of society continued to be the yeoman cultivator, who could turn warrior at will, and there is still little evidence for a disproportionately wealthy exploiting class.

This was the fifth century. While in Greece the poets, philosophers, and sculptors of Periclean Athens were working for the enrichment of a beautiful and highly organized city state, Britain thus remained a simple agricultural land with scattered farmsteads and infrequent small villages. When looking down on the scatter of post-holes and pits marking the site of one of these modest Celtic farmsteads, it takes an effort to realize that without any very incredible chances its original owner might have found himself in classical Greece and watched the building of the Parthenon.

FIG. 14. Plan of Early Iron Age house, Little Woodbury, Wilts.

An Iron Age farm that well represents for us the kind of simple home achieved by the well-to-do members of the Wessex population stood at Little Woodbury, on the chalk down overlooking the Avon valley a mile or so from the place where the spire of Salisbury cathedral was to rise some sixteen hundred years later. The farmer and his household (which may have included some of the live-stock) lived in a spacious round house (Fig. 14) standing in a circular fenced compound among the minor buildings and equipment of the farmyard. The busiest time to visit such a settlement would be the autumn. Then one could see the heads of corn carefully reaped with small sickles and hung on lines stretched between pairs of wooden posts. When the sun and wind had dried them, the grain would be winnowed in shallow depressions in the chalk, then divided into two parts, the larger for winter food, the smaller to be reserved as seed for the coming season. This seed corn, on which the hopes of the next season depended, had very special care, being stored in little square granaries, well ventilated and raised above the dampness of the ground. The other part of the crop, that which was intended for food, was dried in clay ovens to prevent germination before being poured for storage into deep, chalk-cut pits, roofed over and lined with basketry or skins. As grain-stores these pits had a short life, for after a few years they became infected with moulds and had to be abandoned: they were then commonly converted into rubbish-tips and filled with ashes, bones, and all manner of domestic litter. During the course of some three centuries no fewer than three hundred and sixty such pits were sunk in the compound at Woodbury.

A household of this kind would be able to cultivate about 15 acres of arable, of which only one half or one third would be sown in any one year, while the downland grass offered good pasture for flocks of a small breed of sheep and a herd of short-horn cattle. Below in the wooded valley pigs could find a living, and the farmer bring variety to his table by hunting red-deer and other smaller game.

Farm equipment included the two-ox plough, perhaps now sometimes shod with iron, iron sickles, and querns for grinding flour by rubbing a smaller stone to and fro on a larger one.

Cloth was more than ever in demand, and the women must often have been sitting outside the house spinning yarn with the help of simple bone, pottery, or stone spindle whorls, or inside weaving at their looms with a line of triangular clay weights dangling from the warp threads. To separate and control these threads and to press down the woof they used well-made bone combs with long, decorated handles. Unhappily we shall probably never know the colour or designs of the fabrics cut from these Iron Age looms, nor much about the style of the clothes for which they were intended.

The craft of potting, too, achieved a much higher standard than anything known in Britain before. Now for the first time there is the sharp distinction to which we have since grown accustomed between the 'best' service and the coarser kitchen ware. The fine crockery included shapely and thin-walled bowls (Fig. 15), some with simple geometric decoration

FIG. 15. Early Iron Age pottery bowl from Little Woodbury, Wilts.

cut on a glossy red surface. This attractive red colouring was obtained by dipping the pots in the iron oxide known as haematite to form a coating which was afterwards highly polished in imitation of bronze. One can imagine such bowls ranged on a shelf in an Iron Age farmhouse warmly lit by the fire and looking almost as attractive as a dresser full of old lustre.

The manufacture of such pieces demanded a special skill and knowledge which could hardly belong to the ordinary housewife. It was, in fact, carried on by experts, who seem to have traded their wares over quite wide areas. The simple cooking utensils, on the other hand, were made at home out of the local clays, although the women often strove to imitate in this crude medium the elegant form of the bronze bucket (p. 110).

Iron seems to have been used only sparingly, or at least was

carefully husbanded, for little is ever found in the early settlements: a few knives, pins, rings, or other small objects being the
most that remain.

Not all the Early Iron Age population can have lived in
isolated farms such as Little Woodbury. Their dwellings
may sometimes have clustered together on lower ground in
groups that might be called villages, but at present such settlements have not been certainly identified for this period. If they
did exist, they were not nearly so common as we used to suppose
when every grain-store was believed to represent a 'pit-dwelling', so that Little Woodbury would have been mistaken for
a village of over three hundred houses! On this subject archaeologists have waged a stubborn battle. Clearly the imaginative
appeal of the pit-dwelling is very great: there is something of
the romantic savage in the picture of our ancestors passing
their lives crouched in holes 10 feet below the ground. So
great, indeed, is it that for long its supporters were blind to the
evident truth that no human being could linger over a fire in
such a pit and emerge alive. Cold reason, however, has been
accepted in the end and banished the pit-dwellers from our
history; instead it is recognized that these peasants had a
practical means for storing the winter food necessary to support
their increasing numbers.

As well as open villages there were strongholds on many
hills, especially among the chalk downs of the south. The
defences were slight enough at first – often a wooden palisade
following the contours of the hilltop. Such places were probably intended primarily as temporary refuges for times of
danger, even if farmers may sometimes have chosen to settle
more permanently within their protective walls. Though
unambitious in structure, these refuges already indicate a fair-
sized social group united for its own security. And before long
there were happenings which made such defence an imperative
necessity.

While the Hallstatt Celts were quietly digging themselves

into British soil, the expansion of the Celtic peoples had been causing widespread disturbance on the Continent. In the fourth century before Christ, Celts crossed the Alps, conquered territory in Italy, and sacked Rome; by the third they were pushing farther eastward, fighting the Macedonians, assailing Delphi, and even crossing into Asia Minor, where they were to settle and become the 'foolish Galatians' of St Paul. Nor, as we have just hinted, did the West escape. In this same century their warrior bands crossed the Channel and caused panic among the population of Britain. With them into Britain they brought a culture that can no longer be called Hallstatt. Already when the first Hallstatt settlers were arriving in this country their kinsfolk in eastern France and south Germany were building up a new culture, that known as La Tène, which came to represent the height of early Celtic achievement. The Celts of these regions were helped to make this development from their old Hallstatt civilization by the stimulating contacts which they were receiving from the Mediterranean – particularly from the Etruscans of Italy and the prosperous Greek colonists of Marseilles. The Celts sent south such goods as backward peoples can usually supply to their more advanced neighbours, slaves and raw materials, above all metals, furs, and amber from farther north. In exchange they imported a Mediterranean product for which they had developed a passionate desire: wine. With this wine came all the equipment for its proper enjoyment, fine bronze and pottery vessels for its carriage, storage, mixing, and drinking. Chiefs might afford a whole table service of bronze wine vessels, many of which would be enriched with the stylized plant designs of classical convention. In this manner such patterns came before the eyes of the Celtic artist-craftsmen who were presently fired to adopt them as foundations for their own work. So that it has truly been said that 'La Tène art may largely have owed its existence to Celtic thirst.'

But no barbarian could merely imitate a Greek. The Celts

soon transformed these borrowed conventions, with others that reached them from the Scythians of south-eastern Europe, into something inimitably their own; the orderly human spirit of classical taste fled before the free, flamboyant, visionary spirit which now inspired barbarian genius, to yield at last one of the most masterly abstract arts which Europe has known.

These good wines and lovely objects were for the gratification of a wealthy warrior aristocracy, for men such as those whose richly furnished graves are known by the Middle Rhine and in the Marne region of France. There they lay below covering mounds, buried in full pomp with lavishly ornamented sword and helmet, with their wine-flagons and their fighting chariots. It seems that it was about 250 B.C. that numbers of such warriors began, as we have seen, to cross to Britain, sailing probably from the mouth of the Seine, and introduce for the first time the La Tène culture which was to bear its final and most mature fruits in these islands.

The consternation which their coming provoked among the population was not without some practical results. The inhabitants began hastily to throw up defence works; farmers, such as the owners of Woodbury, dug ditches round their homesteads and strengthened their fences, while hilltops were crowned with quite formidable forts, sometimes replacing the older palisaded strongholds (p. 123). Hardly less familiar landmarks than the long and round barrows are these 'camps' which crown so many of our hills, their defences following the natural contours. Probably many of the earliest were put up at this time in the third century before Christ against the inroads of La Tène warriors from the Continent. Their building was a formidable effort, even more formidable than their present appearance suggests. To-day, though impressive in scale, they look simple enough (Pl. 15): a single turf-covered bank sloping gradually into a mild, grassy ditch: from a distance no more than a tiny nick in the profile of the hill. But this form is the outcome of collapse and decay. Picture them as they were when new-built and ready for defence. The attacker was first confronted with a steep-sided ditch cut deep into the chalk; beyond lay a narrow strip of level ground under direct fire from the ramparts, which presented an almost sheer wall of timbers or coursed turf or stone secured by stout uprights. Against the back of this revetment the chalk bank was piled, its top making a protected rampart wall for the defenders. At the weakest point in the circuit, the entrance, the rampart might swing inwards so that the wooden gates stood inset at the end of a funnel-like entry which could be raked by crossfire.

One can imagine the scene so well – the dead white of the newly dug chalk, the raw feel and smell of the fresh timber, the wood-chippings scattered on the trampled ground.

So sudden and short were the onsets of danger that these early forts were often abandoned unfinished, and few were occupied for long. The determined and organized resistance to aggression which they represent discouraged the La Tène raiders and prevented them from settling in any force on the southern chalk. Groups of them did settle here and there, certainly in Sussex round the great fort of Cissbury near Worthing, and in places in Wessex and east Kent, and these brought perceptible changes into the old Hallstatt traditions, but no wholly La Tène type of society was established. Other groups seem to have penetrated beyond the Thames – into East Anglia, for example – establishing their power over the Hallstatt peasantry. Here must be the origin of the royal house of the Iceni which was to end bloodily and heroically in the great queen Boudicca.

In Scotland scattered immigration did little to change a native population still mainly living in a belated Bronze Age. It was not until near the beginning of our era that a substantial expansion of peoples from further south introduced more up-to-date ideas. They it was who built the so-called vitrified forts

of Scotland, such as those well known at Castle Law near
Abernethy and Finavon in Angus. It has been shown by practical experiment that this vitrification or fusing of the rock of
which they are built was not deliberate. The forts were in fact
originally built by a method not unlike that which Caesar
found still in use among the Gauls: stone facings were bonded
together with vertical and horizontal timbers, and more wood
went into the rubble core. When such a building was set on
fire, accidentally or by an enemy, the timbers burnt away, and
their sockets made such efficient flues that enough heat was
generated to melt and fuse the stones. The final but uninten-
tional product was a vitrified fort.

But it was in eastern Yorkshire and Lincolnshire that the
newcomers established their most characteristic colonies.
There La Tène chiefs ruled their followers and the native
population with an absolutism that allowed them to maintain
more of their Continental habits and standards. The tribe to
settle in east Yorkshire was probably already that of the
Parisi, certainly there when Ptolemy wrote four centuries later.
Coming as they did from northern France, we can safely
recognize them as an offshoot of the people whose name has
been so conspicuously preserved in that of the French capital.
It is an amusing thought that such an historical link should
exist between the Parisian and the Yorkshire tyke.

In this north-eastern region, more than any other, society
fell into a highly aristocratic pattern, recalling that of the Early
Bronze Age. Wealth and power were concentrated in the
hands of a small minority who formed a world of relative
luxury. In that world it seems that women could occupy a
high and honourable place.

Much thought was given to personal appearance. The men
wore cloaks or plaids fastened at the shoulder with safety-pin
brooches sometimes studded with coral, and hung wrists and
ankles with bronze or jet bangles. With wealth and leisure the
amiable vice of vanity could be cultivated, and we find a La

Tène lady sophisticated enough to employ polished metal hand-mirrors in making her toilet.

The chiefs' weapons were of the finest. They carried iron-bladed daggers, the bronze hilt often in the form of a manikin with splayed arms and legs, and short iron swords sheathed in bronze scabbards that might be richly chased with La Tène designs. For defence they had oval wooden shields with orna-mental mountings in bronze, and perhaps occasionally helmets.

These heroes no longer had to go into battle on foot, but drove in the two-wheeled chariots which the Celts had adopted from the Etruscans of Italy. The chariots were wooden, and had spoked iron-tyred wheels standing rather less than three feet high. By Caesar's time at least, they opened forwards to allow the warrior to dart recklessly down the shaft-pole be-tween the pair of horses when he wished better to reach an adversary or cast a javelin. From snaffle-bits of surprisingly modern design (Pl. 16b) the reins passed through decorated bronze terret rings into the hands of the charioteer, whose duty it was to manoeuvre the vehicle for his warrior master.

When admiring the beauty of La Tène weapons and trap-pings, it is well to remember that the resplendent aristocrats under whose patronage they were made probably passed their everyday lives in squalor. Their houses were of the simplest – round huts lacking in domestic amenities. It was in part this combination of lavish personal display with graceless living that the Greeks and Romans despised in their barbarian neighbours.

In an aristocratic society of this type it is not surprising to find a return to elaborate and expensive funerary rites. The dead were laid in pits below small, round barrows, fully clad and decked with ornaments, and, just as in France, they might be accompanied by their war chariots, sometimes complete, more often dismantled. It was only a very great man who could hope to be furnished with horses; normally they were too valuable for sacrifice, and their harness alone went into the

The greatest contribution to history made by this north-eastern La Tène colony was in the work of its artists. During the centuries which followed its foundation they more than any of their contemporaries were responsible for the growth of a British school of decorative art which is one of the outstanding episodes in the story of our civilization.

Their achievement has mainly to be judged from the metal-work which has survived where a mass of lovely but perishable things must have disappeared. But it is enough to show that these artists happily combined the surest sense of plastic form with an equal mastery of decorative design in the flat. Their plastic skill is admirably shown in the horse-bits already mentioned (Pl. 16b): one feels that aesthetically the craftsman who conceived them could do no wrong. A snaffle-bit like this is wholly practical, yet so perfect are the proportions, the curves, and the mouldings that the whole is a certain work of art. The same mastery can be still better appreciated by studying Pl. 12b, the detail of a bronze sacrificial dish from Celtic Ireland. In surface decoration the earliest style is still based on renderings of classical plant forms, but these were conceived in a Celtic freedom that developed towards a pure geometric style, a style of dynamic pattern, the poise of which stiffened into a duller and more formal symmetry only when touched by the influence of Rome.

One of the loveliest individual masterpieces of the early designers is the sword dredged from the river Witham (Pl. 9). The bronze scabbard mount curls up and over in curves as free and unpredictable as a sea-wave. Another piece designed a little later is the Torrs champfrein or horse's head-armour, a striking object even now we know that originally it was crowned by a plume or panache and not by the bronze horns attached to it in recent times. Though much later in date, the fine bronze mirrors from Birdlip and Desborough (Fig. 20) are evidently part of the same flow of genius, as is also that great national treasure the Battersea shield (Pl. 13), but we shall find that here fresh currents are augmenting the stream (p. 149). This later phase, which led to the final one when British La Tène art was first debased and then suppressed by the alien traditions of Rome, belongs more properly to the next chapter.

Meanwhile, and long before our Celtic art had reached the advanced stage to which we have now followed it, another region of Britain was receiving La Tène immigrants. The motives which took them from west France to south-western England seem to have been rather different from those operating elsewhere. Here in the south-west it was not only to plunder and seize land that they came; they were pursuing trade, even if it was at the sword's point. The tin of west Cornwall had been a major factor in the Bronze Age economics of western Europe, and now once more this peninsula was invaded by warrior traders who saw that its control would bring them wealth. Here we get the first glimpse of recorded British geography. The daring Greek explorer Pytheas visited Cornwall in about 325 B.C., and to him is ascribed the famous account of how its people mined and smelted the tin and brought it across in waggons at low tide to the island of Ictis, whence continental merchants took it by ship to the west French coast, and so overland to the mouth of the Rhône and the markets of Mediterranean civilization. Unless the coastline has changed, Ictis is most likely to be St Michael's Mount, and the trade evidently supported a large mining population in the tin-bearing regions round about and kept them in touch with the Continent.

Conquest and exploitation here meant a rich prize for the La Tène adventurers, and since the earlier inhabitants were not warlike, and probably but little advanced beyond the material level of the Late Bronze Age, the prize may have been easily won. But to secure their hold the invading leaders needed fortified strongholds. We have already seen how the descendants of the Hallstatt people in Wessex and elsewhere built hill-forts against the La Tène invaders of the third century

B.C. The same thing may have been tried here and there against our south-western invaders, but the strongholds which they built for their own security, though standing likewise on hill or upland sites, are forts of a distinctive type, with a strictly circular ground-plan. In west Cornwall such stone-walled ring-forts as Chun Castle are prominent features of the landscape, and often stand above a contemporary hamlet, much as a medieval baron's castle at once protects and overawes its village.

The hamlets here were also distinctive. A typical one, dominated by the fort of Castle-an-Dinas, was that of Chysauster, south-west of St Ives, which lasted from late in this period into Roman times. It had at least eight houses, built on the courtyard plan (p. 112), flanking a cobbled street: these were surrounded by garden plots and small arable fields, and the inhabitants were not only cultivators, but also miners and smelters of tin. Both fort and village dwellers made and used the subterranean galleries which the Cornish know as fogous. These were apparently hiding-places against attack, and, whatever their origin, they go with the forts to show that violence and warfare now loomed large in all men's lives.

Farther east, in Cornwall, there were fewer fogous, but more ring-forts, such as Castle Dore near Fowey, within which the inhabitants dwelt in timber-built round huts. Farther east again, this south-western culture came closer to the main stream of British civilization, and fort-building drew more on the older contour-plan tradition described above (p. 125), issuing presently in imposing new developments.

By the beginning of the first century B.C. the increasingly warlike character of Celtic civilization was in this corner of Britain enhanced by the rise of a new weapon, the sling. With this simple loop of leather, a man could hurl a smooth pebble or a baked clay bullet with great force at comparatively long range, to smite his enemy as David smote Goliath, and organized companies of slingers could play as deadly a part in battle as riflemen in more modern warfare. The art of the sling came probably along the tin route from the western Mediterranean, where for example Balearic slingers were so famous, and the development of the art of fortification to suit it was apparently begun by the Veneti, the coastal people of Brittany who plied most of the cross-Channel trade with south-western Britain. The main feature was to multiply the number of your lines of defence, to set the greatest possible distance between yourself inside them and the attacking enemy outside. This multiplication of ramparts was, it seems, first applied to the 'cliff castles' with which these people fortified the promontories of their rocky coast, and the application was perhaps first generally made when all ancient France or Gaul was invaded by the wild Cimbric and Teutonic tribes from northern Europe, just before 100 B.C. Similar cliff castles, evidently the work of these same Veneti or their British associates, stand thick along the coasts of Cornwall, and the principle of multiple ramparts, suited to sling warfare, was also extended inland, for ring-forts and soon also for hill-top fortresses of larger size, contour-planned in the older native tradition.

The result was a gradual spread of hill-fortification on a great scale, from the south-west northward and eastward, wherever aggression or colonization by the south-westerners, or imitation of them by other tribes, carried the new sling warfare. Neither at first made much headway in Wessex; the famous Maiden Castle near Dorchester, originally a moderate-sized fort of the older native type, was early in this phase enlarged, but with only a single ditch and rampart, and by the Wessex natives, not the south-western aggressors.

It was from Cornwall and Devon coastwise along the Bristol Channel that the new art of war spread mainly. Some groups of trading colonists were probably going this way already, for example to Bredon Hill fort, on the edge of the Cotswolds, but more followed and on both sides of the Severn. The iron of the Forest of Dean was probably one of their major objectives, and there was coastal settlement farther west in Wales, while others began to move northward into the country of the Marches. Presently all this quarter of Britain was by warfare, trade, and migration linked together in a loose cultural unity, of which the forts serve as an abiding sign.

But by far the most remarkable centres of La Tène culture which are known in this region are protected not by fortification, but by water – the Somerset lake-villages of Meare and Glastonbury. These were settled later than the first invasions into Cornwall, and it may well be that further immigrants from Brittany, to be noticed later (p. 148), had a share in their foundation, or at least development; but their excavation has given us an exceptionally full picture of the life of the period. The Glastonbury village, lying about a mile north of the modern town, is the better known. It was excellently placed for trade, being connected by the Mendips with the main upland system of British trackways, and within coastwise reach of the Cornish tin exporters, as well as in direct touch southward with the shores of the Channel. For the security which the stormy times demanded, the founders of the village chose a piece of marshy ground that probably became completely flooded in winter and spring. Well equipped with iron billhooks, they hacked down the growth of alder and willow which cumbered the site, and then, with immense labour, went on to build up an artificial island on the ground they had cleared. Its main bulk was a bed of horizontal logs, close-packed and sometimes as much as 4 feet in thickness, but it was made yet more substantial with clay, stones, brushwood, and bracken, much of which had to be carted from a distance. To prevent it from spreading, they bounded their island with a stout palisade of vertical timbers driven well down into the marsh, the tops projecting to form a strong fence.

At the height of its prosperity this man-made island exceeded 10,000 square yards in extent, and on it stood some sixty round huts with wattled sides, trodden clay floors, and roofs thatched with reeds. Each house had a stone or clay hearth in the centre of the floor, and some had paved doorsteps, while cobbled alley-ways led between them. The village would first appear to the visitor as a huddle of thatched roofs rising among the thickets of alders and willows; carts are bringing produce from the higher ground where the villagers keep their beasts and cultivate corn and vegetables, while dug-out canoes moored at a landing-stage are ready for fowling expeditions among the many waterways, or for longer trading excursions. Inside its protecting wall, the village itself is full of life and activity – a compact stronghold of humanity isolated among the swamps. Duck and coot can be heard calling and splashing among reeds where herons and cranes stand motionless; occasionally a bittern sounds its uncanny, booming call; and there, top-heavy, comical, and grotesquely beautiful, a family of pelicans is sailing down the open waterway. The villagers naturally avail themselves of all this wild life over their fence to add seasonable variety to their meals: they enjoy wild-fowl of many kinds, especially duck, and also such freshwater fish as perch, roach, and trout.

Indeed, in all ways their industry and enterprise gave them a high standard of life. Carpenters were highly skilled and ambitious. Their accomplishments ranged from the heavy work of constructing platforms and houses, and of hollowing canoes, through cart-building and beautiful wheelwright's work, to such delicate operations as the lathe-turning of wooden vessels (Fig. 17) and the carving of ladles and graceful handles for iron implements. This iron equipment was itself varied and efficient. Blacksmiths' designs have changed little through the centuries, and Glastonbury sickles and bill-hooks (Fig. 17) hardly differ from those used to trim our own hedges and ditches, while neat little saws, as well as chisels and gouges, were forged for the carpenters. Bronze still had many uses. A sheet-bronze bowl ornamented with large hollow rivet-heads is one of the prides of Glastonbury town, where somewhat tinny reproductions can be bought as souvenirs – an honour which would surely have surprised and delighted its one-time owners. Among more domestic crafts, weaving was much practised; the same long-handled combs (Fig. 17) were popular as those used by the women of the earlier Iron Age, but an

FIG. 17. The Glastonbury Lake Village: weaving comb, handle, dicebox, billhook, and wooden tub.

improvement of method is shown by the trim little bone bobbins which carried the yarn in wooden shuttles. Another important labour-saving device – invented long since in the East – was the rotary quern for grinding corn. For nearly two thousand years, ever since the introduction of cereals for food in Neolithic times, housewives had been content to make their flour by pushing one stone to and fro over another. Now they had only to turn a handle to revolve an upper stone pivoted in the nether one.

The Glastonbury people – perhaps it was again the women – were excellent potters. Their products are famous among all our prehistoric wares for the rich La Tène decoration which was engraved on smoothly-rounded bowls or fat, comfortable-looking pots rather like Chinese ginger-jars. The incised patterns are often both ingenious and pleasing, though a certain stiffness is introduced by the frequent use of compasses in laying out the designs – a matter to which we shall return below (p. 149). When the wheel principle was in use not only for vehicles and for querns, but even for turning wooden vessels, it is surprising to find that the fast-turning potter's wheel was apparently still unknown. The Glastonbury villagers have perhaps been made to sound excessively industrious; but they were not above gambling, with dice to throw from carefully carved boxes (Fig. 17). Probably the strongest impression one gets from the village is that the art which had formerly been enjoyed only by the Celtic aristocracy had here spread, simplified in form but still admirable in taste, to the common people and their everyday works and surroundings.

Their general standard of culture was perhaps unusually high, for they were evidently much of a trading community, importing Cornish tin, lead from Mendip, Dorset shale, glass beads and amber from the Continent, and, probably mainly from the Forest of Dean, much iron, which went not only to make tools, weapons, and useful appliances of many kinds, but to furnish the medium of commerce itself – that is, a currency. This took the form of long, flat iron bars (Fig. 18), pinched up at one end, perhaps derived from the roughouts for sword-blades, but standardized in weight. They must have been very cumbersome to handle, but are found here and over a wide area in the south-west of Britain, testifying further to its unity of culture, and to its outside connexions also, since they extend into Wessex, the Thames valley, and the Midlands. The way across the Midland forests was marked by the belt of Jurassic rock-subsoil which makes a corridor of open country from the Cotswolds over into Lincolnshire, and there is an important ring-fort on the line at Hunsbury near North-ampton, where the local ironstone was worked and a variety of remains shows a culture very like that of the Somerset villages, though it began earlier and did not survive as late. This way went the main connexions with the north, where the Parisian and other La Tène peoples were still flourishing, their more distant venturers now even reaching the north of Ireland.

FIG. 18. Iron currency-bars of the Iron Age.

And the other way went the connexions with the Continent across the western end of the Channel, where the sailing-galleys of the Veneti plied between Britain and Brittany. Though an iron anchor and its chain are known from a fort near Poole Harbour, actual remains of those galleys have never yet been found. But their description has come down to us, written by the man who brought their power to an end. That man was Julius Caesar, the Roman conqueror of Gaul, who in 56 B.C. met the defiance of the tribes of Brittany in a great sea battle off their coast, and utterly destroyed their assembled fleet. The next year he addressed himself to the invasion of Britain.

CHAPTER 6

Britain and the Romans

It may seem strange to the English reader, for whom going abroad has usually meant Dover to Calais, that the broad Atlantic end of the Channel should ever have served for a main crossing between his island and the Continent. But this Brittany crossing was, of course, part of the ancient Atlantic sea-route, and it connected the metal-bearing west with the easiest ancient way to the markets of the Mediterranean, past the mouth of the Loire and across south-west France. On the other hand, the Straits of Dover, until near the end of pre-historic times, lay between regions not particularly wealthy or important in themselves, and not particularly connected with the more distant centres of European civilization. Only when occasional major folk-movements broke into the sequestered corner of France did they bear any very distinguished traffic. But as the Iron Age wore on, major folk-movements became more frequent and more formidable; in particular, while the Mediterranean civilization that became the Roman Empire was spreading from the south, the Germanic peoples had begun to press down from the north. Their climate had been getting colder and wetter, and, with better farming and the introduction of iron, their population bigger and their armament stronger. One of their outlets was across the Rhine in this direction.

As early as the Late Bronze Age, pressure this way had been one of the causes of Celtic migration to Britain, and by the time the Cimbric and Teutonic tribes mentioned in the last chapter broke through into Gaul and beyond, there had been much Germanic infiltration among the Celts of the Low

Countries, and a mixed Celtic population also with a Germanic tinge had succeeded to the older La Tène culture of the Marne (p. 125). These peoples were called Belgae, and at the beginning of the first century B.C. they had spread west to cover most of the country between the lower Rhine and the lower Seine with their own latter-day version of La Tène civilization. The lands directly across the Straits from Britain were thus drawn into that civilization much more fully than before, and their population increased. At the same time German aggression moved south and grew stronger. Presently the Celtic tribe of the Helvetii, pressed between the upper Rhine and the Swiss Alps, could bear it no longer, and determined to migrate in a body towards the west. Their departure would have left a great breach for German entry into Gaul; and it is at this point, in 55 B.C., that Julius Caesar arrives upon the scene.

The growing power of the Romans had some time before annexed what is now the south of France, and Caesar's object now was not only to keep the Germans out, but to annex the whole country for Rome. Ultimately, he succeeded. We have already seen how in the course of his famous campaigns he conquered the Veneti of Brittany. But the Belgae in the north-east had given him much hard fighting in the previous year, and he had not been at this long before he found that they were being helped from Britain, where, just across the Straits of Dover, they had kinsmen of their own, who had migrated thither less than a generation before. The Belgae, in fact, had overflowed into south-eastern Britain, and had made the lands they had settled provinces of Belgic culture.

Remains of this Belgic culture have often been discovered. The Belgae, like the Germans, cremated their dead, and they buried the ashes in shapely urns, usually pear-shaped and often with a pedestal foot, which are sometimes found grouped in cemeteries or urnfields. The best known are in Kent, where they settled first: Swarling, near Canterbury, and Aylesford on the Medway. In most graves the urn was accompanied by other pots, no doubt to hold funeral offerings of food and drink, and sometimes by bronze or even silver brooches, shaped like a large and ornate safety-pin. At Aylesford there were also bronze vessels – a pan and wine-jug – from Italy, and a great wooden bucket bound and handled in bronze, with two un-earthly-faced human heads frowning above the rim, and designs beaten out on the upper band, including strange, leafy-tailed horse-monsters. Here we have a fresh instalment of La Tène art from Gaul; yet it is not for such isolated treasures that the Belgae are most notable, but rather for their more efficient and better-equipped mastery of the arts of everyday life.

They made pottery on the true potter's wheel; their ironwork, of which there will be more to say presently, was superlative, as was their woodwork also, and in addition to warlike and domestic gear they made a new type of plough, built on more advanced lines and armed with a big coulter to cut the sod and allow a deeper furrow. Whereas the old, light, two-ox plough could only drive a superficial furrow even in easy soils, this new plough enabled them to till comparatively heavy ground, which they could first clear of timber with their iron axes; and so there began something of a revolution in British agriculture and land settlement. Thus, while the scattered farmsteads in which they mainly lived were still primitive as dwellings – simple round or oval huts for the most part – their produce nourished a thriving population. And Belgic fighting strengh carried still farther the dominance of warfare over Iron Age life. They fought on foot, on horse-back, and from chariots, and though they had not developed the same art of multiple fortification as the western peoples, they could make formidable hill-forts enough, on woodland sites for choice, with defences often relying especially on a steep and wide main ditch. And in twenty years from their first coming they had spread from Kent to the Thames, and from the Thames deep into northern Hertfordshire.

Caesar himself contrasted the civilized life of south-eastern

England with the more barbaric ways of the interior: 'Of the inlanders, most do not sow corn, but live on milk and flesh and clothe themselves in skins.' This was long thought to be a gross exaggeration of our insular barbarity due only to lack of information. Now, however, it is recognized that Caesar's statement is at least partially true. There was a fundamental difference between the way people lived north and south of a frontier running roughly from Bath to Lincoln. To the north of it agriculture played only a small part in the economy and the tribes depended on ranching, all wealth coming from great numbers of cattle and many sheep. Even at the fortress at Stanwick in Yorkshire, built by the Brigantian prince Venutius against the Roman conquerors over a century later, the population evidently still depended almost entirely on livestock and ate little grain. Thus all through the Celtic centuries we have to think of Britain falling into two economic provinces with farming practice differing almost as sharply as today it does between East Anglia and the Welsh hills.

Caesar's judgement of the situation was that the security of a conquered Gaul demanded a conquered Britain. Accordingly, in August 55 B.C. he made a start by crossing from Boulogne with some 10,000 men, to explore, and, if all went well, to force obedience at least on the Belgae of eastern Kent. But all did not go well: his fleet was damaged by a stormy high tide on the beach near Deal, and the local tribes with their chariots and horsemen gave his army some very sharp encounters. He therefore got the expedition back to Gaul as soon as he could, and prepared for a larger one next year. Elaborate preparations were made, and about midsummer he crossed again, with a much larger force; he struck inland at once, and stormed the Belgic hill-fort of Bigbury near Canterbury – but only to learn that his fleet had once more been damaged by a storm. While it was being repaired, the Kentish tribes allied themselves with the leading Belgic chieftains beyond the Thames in Hertfordshire. This was Cassivellaunus, an aggressive leader, against whom Caesar's assistance had already been sought by one of the non-Belgic tribes, the Trinovantes, who lived in Essex. Cassivellaunus knew he could not withstand the Roman legions in a pitched battle, but by skilful mobile warfare he harassed their advance over Kent, and again after they had crossed the Thames and reached the Trinovantes. At last Caesar found and stormed his hill-fort capital at Wheathampstead; but even then the Romans had to beat off a fresh onslaught by his Kentish allies on their naval base. By early autumn he came to terms; but though Caesar imposed on him an annual tribute, and a promise to leave the Trinovantes alone, the great Roman general retired to Gaul aware that Britain had really not been conquered at all. The fame of Cassivellaunus' resistance lived on ever afterwards in British story, but Caesar soon found that to conquer Gaul itself he needed several more years of bitter fighting, while he had only marked down Britain for conquest in the future.

Caesar's account of his invasions and of Britain generally, given us in his famous *Commentaries*, is the earliest surviving piece of written history concerned with our island. But he did not get beyond one corner of it, and by setting what he has told us against a background of modern knowledge, we can fill out his picture in many ways. It is clear that through the Belgic colonization, the corner which he visited had for the first time become the most powerful and most civilized, as civilization then went. It is clear also that the non-Belgic inhabitants hated and feared the Belgae, and opposed their expansion. The Trinovantes were even glad to take sides with Caesar against Cassivellaunus, and between Wheathampstead, their enemy's capital fortress, and St Albans, where his successors presently settled, a great Belgic boundary ditch may still be seen, along the valley known as Beech Bottom. To dig this 100 feet wide and over 30 feet deep as they did, the intruders must indeed have been uneasy at first in their adopted land. The Wheathampstead fortress ditch is even bigger, and the tale of hostility between the Belgae and their neighbours is not confined to Hertfordshire.

In Kent their southern flank ran along the wooded fringes of the Weald, and here the inhabitants protected themselves against them by building large hill-forts like Oldbury Camp near Ightham. These inhabitants were largely an offshoot of the earlier La Tène immigrants into Sussex, whose expansion over the Wealden forest was no doubt connected with its important deposits of iron ore. There is evidence that the Kentish Belgae also worked Wealden iron, while, as we shall see, their fellows north of the Thames ultimately reached the ironstone region of Northants and Oxfordshire. From the ores thus won, reduced in clay-built furnaces, the Belgic smiths forged their weapons of war, their chariot- and harness-fittings, their implements of forestry and farming, and the furnishings of their chieftains' hearths. These last were superb iron firedogs rising at either end to the likeness of a knob-horned ox-head, which display a true artist's feeling for fitness of design in wrought metal (Pl. 16a). But the westerners' iron bar-currency, which they met with in the Thames valley and beyond, they did not make, for they brought with them from Gaul what was perhaps the most momentous of all the inventions adopted by La Tène from Mediterranean civilization – coinage.

Celtic coinage on the Continent was imitated from Greek, and in central Gaul was first minted in the second century B.C. Early in the next century gold coins of the Belgic Gauls began to circulate in south-east Britain, first those of the Bellovaci (from the district where Beauvais still preserves their tribal name), and then, starting in Kent, where the earliest Belgic colonists settled, those of the Atrebates (from the district of Arras). Such Gaulish types may sometimes have been actually minted over here, and the first distinguishably British coins took their type from an Atrebatic model. The designs of both faces look quite extraordinarily meaningless, until one sees them and their Gaulish models side by side with the Greek type from which they were ultimately derived (Fig. 19). This was the standard gold coin of the famous King Philip of Macedonia (the father of Alexander the Great), and it has on one side the head of the god Apollo wearing a laurel wreath, and on the other a driven chariot with two horses. The successive Celt imitators, to whom the whole idea was strange, reduced both designs in time to uncouth patterns, the head perishing in a maze of blobs crossed by a sort of herring-bone version of the wreath, and the chariot and pair broken up into another maze of blobs, in which one can just see the dismembered skeleton of what once was a horse. But gradually after that the head design was worked out in Britain into a regular cross-pattern,

FIG. 19. Ancient British coins and (on extreme left)
one of their Greek models.

based on the old wreath. And the never quite forgotten horse on the other side was suddenly created afresh, prancing in a weird but animated life. The famous White Horse of Uffington (Pl. 15) is probably a gigantic rendering of the same new form of strange, half-supernatural creature, cut in the chalk of the Berkshire Downs by a people who boasted him as a tribal or religious emblem. And that brings us back to our main story. For this people were at least in part fresh Belgic settlers from Gaul, who, when Caesar was at last victorious there, would not submit to Roman rule, but took refuge in Britain instead.

Caesar in both his expeditions had used the services of the king of the Atrebates, whose name was Comm or Commius. He was a person of some standing not only in Gaul, but in Britain, where we have seen his people's coinage circulating in Kent. Later he turned against Caesar, and when the Gaulish resistance was broken he fled to Britain, with shiploads of followers. This was about 50 B.C., and in due course coins inscribed with the name of Commius are found in Britain; not indeed in Kent, where one would not expect him after his association with the hated Roman, but farther west. There, between the west Sussex coast and the middle Thames, they follow after those with the new type of horse from Gaul just mentioned, and also a local version of the coinage of his own tribe, the Atrebates. It looks as if Atrebatic and other refugees from Gaul settled in these regions in various tribal groups – the new horse on the coins was perhaps contributed by Remi from the district of Reims – which Commius eventually made into a single kingdom.

Like their relatives in the south-east, these people were not only stout warriors: they introduced improved farming and other peaceful arts, and their coins replaced the old native currency of iron bars. Their pottery was made on the wheel, and it is by this that the remains of their settlements are most easily recognized. But, unlike the south-eastern Belgae, they came as survivors of a culture broken by the conquest of their homes, and thus it is natural to find its potters' art reduced among them to a much-diminished range, the commonest type of vessel being a simple bowl or jar with a plain beading for a rim. Such bowls were also used as urns for burying the ashes of their cremated dead.

Commius seems to have died about 20 B.C., and by then the new Belgic lands probably stretched into Wessex as far west as the river Test and beyond it into Wiltshire. They included the Isle of Wight, but the chief harbour was by Chichester, where the first landings had probably been, thirty years before. Here there is a regular series of defensive ditches suggesting the Belgic manner (p. 141), and it must have been the Belgae who brought the native occupation to a sudden end at the old hill-fort of the Trundle, overlooking Goodwood racecourse on the downs above. Then farther inland they had wrecked the native fort on St Catharine's Hill above Winchester by fire, and taken for their own the native settlements on the neighbouring downs, as they did the virgin site of Winchester itself. Apart from a few fortified capitals, the Belgae needed hill-strongholds themselves only in the frontier lands where they fought continually with the natives to extend their territory.

The natives, for their part, built or renewed hill-forts of their own against them. In Wessex the strong forts characteristic of this time begin just west of the line where the circulation of the Belgic coins before Commius leaves off, the line of the river Test, whose steep-sided, marsh-bottomed valley cuts a frontier like a curving trough across the chalk downs of Hampshire. Their defences are variously planned, but most of them have multiple ramparts and ditches, such as we have already seen introduced into the south-west by the Veneti from Brittany, and some have a more or less circular plan like the south-western ring-forts. Where such works are renewals of abandoned earlier forts, they may form a strong citadel inside the old rampart, as at Bury Hill and Danebury near Andover, or, else, as at Yarnbury Castle north-west of Salisbury, an enlarged circuit surrounding it. The farther one goes west, the longer the inhabitants were able to withstand Belgic encroachment, and the more imposing are the forts. The grandest of all is the renowned Maiden Castle in Dorset, where the earlier fort, already enlarged (p. 133), was now transformed (Pl. 14): the new multiple works brought its size to close on 100 acres, and the inner rampart, towering at least 50 feet above the bottom of its fronting ditch, was massively built in chalk and earth and clay and limestone masonry, the limestone laboriously brought from outcrops over two miles away. The entrance defences were as complex as they were formidable, and the 45 acres of the space within made now no mere occasional camp of refuge, but a permanently inhabited township, the capital of the nameless chief whose will raised this stupendous fortress.

His domain was 70 miles westward from the first footholds of the Belgae on the Chichester coast, and they did not reach and conquer it for some seventy years. The military architecture which served to hinder them so long was, in fact, first brought to central Dorset by more western folk from Gaul, conceivably including the remnant of the Breton Veneti themselves, when Caesar had broken their power across the Channel in 56 B.C. Like their relations earlier in Cornwall and along the Severn Sea, they were warrior adventurers, and with their swords and spears and deadly sling-stones they forced themselves by conquest upon the natives, and secured their hold in these great forts, just as the Norman conquerors of later England did in their castles. In any case, the farming life of the countryside went on virtually unaltered, and the round houses and granary store-pits of the traditional sort were still made much as before. But a new kind of pottery was being made in the Dorset region at this time, with bowls and jars with a bead-rim rather like the Belgic, but of simpler form, and made without the potter's wheel, often with loop handles sunk in the body on either side.

These territories shared in the general south-western circuit of trade and metal-working, and they used the iron bar-currency, but later took to coinage modelled on the Belgic. By then the neighbouring Dobunni, as the people of the Cotswolds and the lower Severn were called, had begun to issue coins bearing the names of kings, with designs based on Belgic models, and the Iceni of the eastern counties, and the Brigantes centred in western Yorkshire, had done the same. The coins of the Dorset people were uninscribed, but we know that their tribal name was the Durotriges.

The Belgae and the warrior invaders from Northern Gaul with their possible Venetic element, were not the only groups of people to be driven across from Gaul in these times. There were also minor groups, and these included immigrants who had something of their own to contribute to the growth of the old La Tène style into a distinctively British Celtic art.

The scribing of geometrical forms of La Tène design on pottery with compasses, helped out by small circle-stamps, was practised in parts of Brittany before Caesar's conquest, and rather similar designs were now brought over, to the Glaston-bury lake-village (Fig. 17) and other places, notably in East Sussex and parts of Kent. Their influence probably helped the development of the curving La Tène scroll-patterns into a purely geometrical style. In this style, on pottery and still more strikingly on fine bronze-work, we find the unfaltering curves and circles of such designs set off by hatching with the look of basketry – though it was more probably inspired by the stitch-ery of gay textiles, which themselves, of course, have perished. The best-established schools of fine bronze-work in Britain were in the northern and eastern territories, where the La Tène style had been implanted by the Parisi and their like (p. 127), but this geometric tendency was furthered from the south, and the results appear in various regions, especially along the connecting line across the Midlands (p. 138) between south-west and north-east.

They appear on ornamented sword-scabbards, as found at Hunsbury (p. 138) and in Somerset near the Meare lake-village, and on a number of smaller things, but most perfectly on the bronze mirrors which we spoke of in the last chapter. Their engraved backs show a varied range of these ingenious spreading curve-patterns, but the most successful are those from

Desborough in the Midlands (Fig. 20) and Birdlip at the Cotswold edge above Gloucester, in which symmetry keeps the
design from straggling without spoiling its grace. As time went
on, symmetry became more and more sought after, and it is
not hard to see in this the first-fruits of a new influence in
British art, the classical influence of Rome. For Gaul was now a

FIG. 20. The Desborough mirror, showing the
engraved ornament of the back.

Roman province, and in the last fifteen years before Christ renewed contacts across the Channel began to bring that influence in. One can admire it, rendered in skilfully cast relief, in the taut, springy formality of our great masterpiece, the shield found in the Thames at Battersea (Pl. 13). But in some of the mirrors it is less admirable, and the nature of its effects can be judged particularly well in the school of ornament centred among the Belgae, which specialized not in line-drawing on metal so much as in enamel-work. In earlier times enamel had been an attached embellishment on metal-work, like the coral which it imitated, but the Belgic craftsmen poured it molten into prepared spaces in their designs, at first in roundels of various kinds like those on the Battersea shield, and then in hollowed-out fields in the ornamental surface itself. Their enamel colour was red, which contrasted showily with the yellow of the bronze; but the effect of Roman influence on their designs was to make them more tidy and correct-looking, like that of the harness-mount from Polden Hill on the Somerset edge of western Belgic territory (Pl. 12b), and in the end fussy or merely clever.

But we have not yet reached the last years of British independence to which these pieces belong. For two full generations from about 20 B.C. the power of the Belgic kingdoms in the south of Britain grew, and rivalry and conflict sharpened, especially between that founded by Commius south of the Thames and that of the successors of Cassivellaunus north of it. Commius had three sons, and their history can be made out in some sort from their coins, which can be arranged in order of age in their various districts, and almost from the outset show the influence of Roman models. The dominion of Cassivellaunus in Hertfordshire descended to a king named Tasciovanus; his coinage, showing the same influence in its own way, was minted mainly at Verulamium, the settlement by St Albans where he had his chief capital. The terms imposed by Caesar were a dead letter now, and he soon resumed aggression against the Trinovantes, which reached its goal when he died about A.D. 10. For his son at once attacked their king (who took refuge with the Roman emperor Augustus) and annexed their capital and lands. The capital was named Camulodunum, where now is Colchester in north-east Essex, and the son, who became the greatest of the British kings, was named Cunobelin – the Cymbeline of Shakespeare's play.

This act of conquest had far-reaching consequences. The Trinovantes had already received Belgic culture and settlers from Kent, and when Cunobelin combined their territory with all his father's dominions he was master of a large and solid kingdom. By about A.D. 25 he had added to it all Kent, and carried his frontier on the north and west to the edge of the Fens and across Northants and Oxfordshire to the Thames, which divided him from the rival kingdom of the house of Commius. At first sight his capital far away in Essex seems an odd choice, but the Colne estuary made Colchester a port, and under him it quickly attracted trade with the Roman Empire across the Narrow Seas. It was now, too, that the first small trading-station was established, probably by Roman merchants, on the site of London. A great military disaster in A.D. 9 had broken the Romans' plan of conquering Germany, and for their merchants the growth of commerce with Cuno-belin's Britain could partly offset the loss of German markets. The Britons exported corn and cattle, metals and also slaves – the captives of their wars, whose iron shackles have several times been found – and received as imports luxuries such as glass and fine pottery, which prepared their material culture for its predestined end – absorption in the Roman Empire itself.

These foreign goods – red-glazed pottery from Italy and its imitations from Belgic Gaul, the great jars which held southern wine, and ornaments such as brooches and the like – have been found in plenty in the central area of Cunobelin's capital, which lay just outside modern Colchester looking onto the river; the native products, pottery above all, were profoundly affected by their example, and on this mounting material civilization the British king grew rich. And on the excellent coinage which he minted, in gold, silver, and bronze, the designs show a positive invasion of Britain by Roman art. The full extent of Camulodunum was immense, though its inhabited areas were scattered, and it was defended on the landward side by line upon line of great dykes of earthwork, much of which may still be seen. Near one of these, at Lexden, was a cemetery of many graves, and here stands a huge barrow, which has been excavated and found to contain a mass of furnishings for the splendour of the dead. There seems to have been a great funeral bier of wood and iron, with lavish ornaments of enamel-studded bronze; the many bronze objects include statuettes in almost wholly classical style, and there was actually a silver portrait-medallion of the Roman Emperor Augustus, made from a coin. This may, indeed, well be the sepulchre of Cunobelin himself.

Exactly what religious beliefs were bound up with such funeral rites is difficult to say, but it appears here, as in many Celtic graves, particularly on the Continent, that grave-goods had been damaged so that they too should be accounted dead, and thus be available for their owner's use beyond the grave. As we have seen, the bodies of the dead were now cremated, and it was certainly the disembodied soul of a man which was held immortal: its passage at death into a new and different body was part of the doctrine taught by the powerful Celtic priesthood of both Gaul and Britain, the order of the Druids. Caesar and other writers have left an account of the Druids which has appealed greatly to people's imagination, and at one time almost every prehistoric monument was thought to be 'Druidical'. Actually their human burnt-offerings, their blood-sacrifices, their divination, their philosophy, and their power as teachers and judges are difficult to place in a modern account of ancient Britain, mainly because the religious monuments of the Iron Age, when they flourished, are so little known. It seems probable that their lore combined traditions coming from a wide range of origins: the cutting of the mistletoe on the sacred oak, for example, was a German as well as a Celtic ceremony, though the golden sickle they are said to have used was perhaps directly descended from the sickles of the Bronze Age in Britain and Gaul. But their development as an organized priesthood seems confined to these western lands, and probably has at least some of its roots in the religious life of the Bronze Age. We have seen that in that life elements brought in by the Beaker and other invaders blended with the mysterious cults of the megalith-builders. Thus, while it is quite wrong to think of Stonehenge as properly a 'Druids' Temple', it is not at all impossible that the Druids may have made use of Stonehenge, then already a venerable monument. But there are no signs of architectural activities at this time: the Iron Age is represented only by scraps of pottery. Near Frilford in Berkshire remains of a little Iron Age sanctuary are known from excavation which looks very like a shrunken and distorted version of an Early Bronze Age 'henge'. Druidism, in fact, though its institutions probably differed in different parts of Britain as regards details, was compounded with ancient elements which the whole land, for all its multitude of gods and goblins, held to some extent in common. And thus it must have been something of a unifying force among the Britons, in an age when local tribes and cultures, invading or invaded, were making such a welter of strife with one another.

The strife was not confined to the frontiers between the Belgae and their neighbours. We have already seen how Cunobelin extended his kingdom by war. Later he seems to have sent his sons with expeditions across the Thames, to carve out princedoms from the lands of the house of Commius. Another expedition had started westwards across north Oxfordshire, where Belgic dyke-building is again in evidence in Blenheim Park, to be repeated by the Dobunni at the im-

portant settlement at Bagendon, near Cirencester, and elsewhere in the Central Cotswolds. Perhaps we can trace the
expansion of these Bulgicized Dobunni much further into the
West Country, where their presence is suggested at a number of
places. The great stone-walled fort of Worlebury at Weston-
super-Mare has yielded many skulls and bones from a massacre,
and at Bredon Hill fort, on the far edge of the Cotswolds, the
main entrance of about this time has been found choked
with the grisly remains of another, in which the victims'
bodies had been hacked to pieces and their heads lined up on
the gate to burn and crash with it to the ground. And the
tremendous hill-forts beyond the Severn, through Hereford-
shire and all up the Marches of Wales, were built and rebuilt,
sometimes on a colossal scale, in a way which shows clearly
enough that the Iron Age of Britain had become truly an age
of iron.

Migrations of peoples in the west went far. Along much of
the west of Scotland there are signs that people now were
coming up from the south, though indeed beyond a few bone
weaving-tools and the like there is little for us now to recognize
them by, except the small, strong ring-forts of their chiefs,
underground galleries like the Cornish fogou (p. 132), and
structures developed from the Cornish courtyard house, which
they seemingly brought with them. But these in the far north
inspired the growth of veritable castles, the towering stone
structures known as brochs (Fig. 21), with stairs and chambers
in the thickness of their walls, and an open court within –
their whole design proclaiming them the strongholds of a
people bred to raiding and fighting by sea and land. Probably
more of such migrations affected Ireland too. Though their
material remains are as yet lacking, the oldest epic tales of
Irish literature reach back to this stage, and tell of a world as
full of the noise of battle as it is full of mystery and magic.

Fighting was, indeed, an accepted part of men's lives in
the ancient world, in civilized Greece no less than in barbaric

Britain. But to both there came a time when war became more than an occasional affair between high-spirited neighbours, and threatened to grow into a perpetual curse. That time came when the pattern of society became too unbalanced for the normal tenor of peace to be maintained, so that war ceased to be a local adjustment of forces, and began to throw the pattern still farther out of balance. New forces were at work, which the

· SECTION · A·D ·

FIG. 21. The Broch of Mousa, Shetland: sectional view showing the stairs and galleries in the walls of the stone tower.

old simple forms of society could not control. The Greek city states could never for long unite, and the civilization they had done so much to create came to demand their merging in something bigger. At long last that something turned into the Roman Empire, and now it was the Roman Empire that came to merge in itself the tribal disunion of Britain.

The Belgic kingdoms had certainly succeeded in merging

lesser tribes, and Cunobelin's was something approaching a national state. But it was the creation of one man, and both the force and the wealth which made the Belgic power rested on their culture's borrowings from the higher civilization overseas. It was not long before the higher civilization was ready to call for the repayment of its debts. Caesar had underrated his task, and had come and gone too soon; but close on a hundred years later the Roman Empire judged that the time was ripe. Soon after A.D. 40 Cunobelin was dead, and his kingdom in turmoil. From his successors' violence the last of the sons of Commius fled to Rome, and the new emperor Claudius saw that the situation demanded a response. Britain was disunited, and had wealth in plenty for exploiting: he had the legions and the ships, and he wanted the laurels of a conquest.

He got them. In the year A.D. 43 a strong Roman army landed on the coast of Kent, and soon Camulodunum surrendered. After forty years of gradual advance by the Romans, their general Agricola at last reached the gate of the Scottish Highlands, and broke in one battle the gathered clans of the northern Britons. But he got no farther. The effort for the Empire was too great, the Highlands were too unrewarding, and the Roman Government thought it best to call a halt. In another forty years there had been a retreat, and Hadrian was building his famous Wall from Tyneside to the Solway. Basing his frontier on that line, he accepted the impossibility of going permanently beyond it, and so it came about that while all the richer lands to the south remained a Roman province, beyond the Wall Prehistoric Britain lived on. Not three centuries from Agricola's day, the Picts and Scots were carrying their warfare back into the province's heart, joining hands with the Saxon invaders from over the North Sea. Soon after A.D. 400 Roman rule in this island was over. And in the 'Dark Ages' which followed, the England, Wales, and Scotland of familiar history were born, with the legacy of Prehistoric Britain, both in war and peace, as a vital part of their inheritance.

Tailpiece

WE started with ape-men, and have ended with Anglo-Saxons. The human history of the half a million or so intervening years has been told, sketchily and laconically in its early parts, but with increasing detail and accuracy. After the first chapter – that is to say, after Britain assumed its island form – the reader may well have been irked by a certain repetitiveness in the story. Chapter after chapter, almost page after page, has shown a recurring theme: the invasion of that island from the Continent. The impact of these waves of invasion beats monotonously through the narrative. From Spain and the Mediterranean, from northern France, the Low Countries, and Scandinavia they roll, each, when it arrives, sweeping over a lesser or a greater part of Britain and altering its character. Often before it reaches the highland zone the force of the wave is spent and it breaks up on the mountain scarps to filter more weakly into the regions beyond.

As writers we regret this monotony, but as prehistorians we cannot alter it. Such was the pattern of British prehistory, a pattern made inevitable by Britain's position as a fertile island accessible to a restless Continental population.

To many the number of these prehistoric incursions may be new and surprising. They may feel incredulous and suspect them to be creations of the archaeologist's imagination. But see how uninterruptedly they run on into historic times, when each has a proper name attached and seems not incredible at all, but simple and familiar. We all know 1066, and before that it was the Danes and Norsemen, then the Anglo-Saxons, the rather different invasion of the Romans, and before them the earliest historically recorded incursion, that of the Belgae. There is no break in continuity and no difference of character between these immigrations and the nameless ones that preceded them. Indeed, the archaeological method has, of course, been applied to the historical invasions, and has given substance and precision to scanty and inaccurate written records.

If this account of early Britain has been monotonous, it has also, we are only too well aware, been full of gaps. These will many of them be closed during the next decade, if anything so essentially peacable as archaeological research is possible in those years. In the present century knowledge has accumulated at an astonishing speed. It was not at first merely a question of closing the gaps, but of setting up the bare framework; incomplete though our information remains, it is immense when compared with the blank which confronted our immediate ancestors when they tried to look back beyond the Roman conquest. A century ago the whole of the time covered by this book was a void vaguely peopled with 'ancient Britons', while the idea that any of these shadowy characters should have been about before 4004 would have seemed dubious to all and blasphemous to many. How and by what manner of men has this information been won? An interest in his own past is perhaps not unexpected in man; it is an obvious field for the exercise of his eternal curiosity, his desire to know. But intellectual inquisitiveness is not the only incentive. There are also the childish pleasures of treasure-seeking which can be given a grown-up form by the cloak of archaeology, and the passion of many individuals for amassing a collection of objects. We have even been told by psychologists that the pursuit of prehistory really represents a striving to return to the womb. These various urges, then, have prompted a number of men and women to devote much time and toil to searching out the remains of the past that survive on and under the surface of their country.

The pioneers were men who travelled the countryside to further the topographical studies which were among the enthusiasms of the English Renaissance. Conspicuous among them was Leland, who in the time of Henry VIII toured England and recorded what he saw of her antiquities, generally medieval castles, abbeys, and the like, but including among them such conspicuous prehistoric monuments as caught his eye and his interest. The Elizabethan age produced Camden, who in 1586 published his bulky volume, *Britannia*, in which was collected a mass of material from medieval writings, but also facts and speculations concerning prehistory. The outstanding figure of the seventeenth century was John Aubrey, an itinerant after the manner of Leland, whose careful field notes are still of the greatest value to present-day students. Even Defoe, preoccupied though he was with commerce, paused to comment on such famous sites as Stonehenge, and incidentally to rebuke the antiquaries of his day for their habit of idle speculation.

All these earlier workers can be seen as the harbingers of the outburst of antiquarian fervour which was one of the results of that great revolution in taste and cultural values, the Romantic Movement. Many of us must have stumbled upon one of those gloomy, dripping, and uncomfortable grottoes dear to the eighteenth- and early nineteenth-century landscape gardener, and read the verses in praise of caves and hermits and ivy inscribed on their walls. To the macabre and morbid side of the Movement prehistoric antiquity was bound to appeal; it could contribute the 'sightless skulls and crumbling bones', the altar stones on which blood might have flowed and victims writhed in 'horrid' fascinating anguish. Above all, it offered a setting for the 'white-haired Druid bard sublime'. The great champion and popularizer of the Druids was William Stukeley, a leader during the earlier phase of the Romantic Movement. In the first decade of the eighteenth century, when he was studying medicine and developing his strong scientific bent, one would have thought him a legitimate child of the Age of Reason, yet he was to end his days as one of the most fantastical of Romantics. Archaeology was at first but one of the many scientific interests which prompted him to keep smelly anatomical specimens in his room at Cambridge and alarm the college with sudden explosions. After 1718, however, when he became first secretary of the newly-formed Society of Antiquaries, it preoccupied him more and more exclusively. At first he used his scientific training to carry out accurate field work, and in particular to survey and plan all the complexities of Avebury and Stonehenge. But gradually another side of his nature better suited to the Romantic taste asserted itself; he grew increasingly fascinated by the Druids, and conceived that he had a mission to reconcile and relate their supposed doctrines with Christianity, and above all with the conception of the Trinity. This change of heart it was which led him to build extravagant theories on the sober and sound foundations of his earlier work at Avebury and Stonehenge, to see in their stone rings and avenues 'a snake proceeding from a circle . . . the eternal procession of the Son from the First Cause'.

Antiquarianism was now the fashion; young gentlemen rode about the country in search of the Gothick and any remains of the more remote past that might present themselves. Landowners began to concern themselves with the monuments they found on their estates. The results of the fashion ranged in value from the careful and exhaustive account of Wiltshire antiquities left by Sir Richard Colt Hoare to the mischievous pillaging of barrows undertaken by a number of gentlemen whose names it is kinder to forget. One among them, rather later, whose ravages can be forgiven him because they were both trivial and picturesque, deserves special place. When this antiquary wished to secure for his collection the contents of a barrow that stood on the property of another, he appeared on the site in an ample cloak and settled down as though to rest or contemplate the beauties of rugged nature. In reality, however, his hands were feverishly busy under the folds of his cloak, excavating the grave and assembling the booty.

As the nineteenth century advanced the social status of archaeology gradually changed in accordance with the changing structure of English society. The power of the upper classes to act as sole arbiters of taste and fashion was slipping from them as the rising middle class assumed control. We find archaeological research passing into the hands of professional or retired business men, and in those hands it was inevitable and right, if a little sad, that the subject should grow more sober and scientific, more in harmony with the gospel of the Prince Consort than it had been in its extravagant youth as a standard-bearer of the Romantic Movement.

In a purely practical way, too, the Industrial Revolution affected archaeology. Never before had the soil of England been so perpetually disturbed, so deeply cut about by the hand of man. Every time that a bank or a factory went up, a canal or railway line was driven, or a quarry sunk, there was good chance that some long-hidden antiquity might be uncovered. To house all these finds, and others the fruits of deliberate archaeological excavation, the middle class subscribed its money to build museums in provincial towns, for it usually lacked both the arrogance and the means which had enabled the eighteenth-century antiquaries to install their collections in their own mansions.

As well as museums, local antiquarian societies were founded. All over the countryside they sprang up, with an enthusiastic membership of squires and doctors and parsons, interested ladies and a few noblemen, all eager to attend and give lectures and to make delightful excursions into the country, armed with notebooks and picnic hampers. It is easy to laugh at them, but these societies have given and continue to give invaluable service to learning. Let anyone who encounters one of their excursions and watches the party, as it turns out of its buses to stream across fields, crowd over stiles, surge into country houses, and toil with limbs often no longer young to the tops of hills, pause and think with some pride of the English tradition which, with all its absurdity, it worthily represents.

Soon after the middle of the nineteenth century archaeology was to be profoundly affected by that happening which did more to liberate the human mind than anything since the day when Galileo realized that the earth went round the sun: the formulation by Darwin of the principles of evolution. Less than a century after the publication of the *Origin of Species* in 1859 it is still hard to appreciate what a tremendous striking off of chains that was. While thinking people had not, of course, always shared the general public's complete acceptance of the 'received' story of the creation and Archbishop Ussher's date for it, nevertheless it narrowly circumscribed their thought.

Into the wide vista of speculation and study finally laid open by Darwin and Huxley, no one was more bound to advance than the archaeologist. Man could now be fitted into geological time, and this aspect of archaeological research developed most rapidly. Immediately the Frenchman Boucher de Perthes' claim to have found humanly shaped implements in early gravels became acceptable, and the Neanderthal skull from Gibraltar, which had lain incognito since its discovery in 1848, was hailed as one of the precursors of Adam, a being who could now be recognized by respectable people.

The half-century after the appearance of the *Origin of Species* was a time of steady progress in archaeological studies. Field workers such as Greenwell and Mortimer in Yorkshire and Cunnington in Wiltshire laboured to produce a mass of factual material on which classifications and generalizations could gradually be built. The great Manchester professor Boyd Dawkins did much to reconcile the geological approaches to archaeology with the humanistic.

Overtopping them all was an unusual and latterly eccentric figure, a figure great enough to be an exception to the main trend of his times. General Lane Fox Pitt-Rivers was a man who would seem more in place among eighteenth-century antiquaries. After a career as a Guards officer he inherited vast estates round Cranborne Chase; he could ride, it was said, from Rushmore to the sea without leaving his own land. Cranborne Chase is scattered with antiquities of many kinds, and the General was now able to satisfy the interest in primitive material culture and excavation which had hitherto been only an immense spare-time hobby. He had many greater eccentricities. He planted his grounds with exotic trees and shrubs and filled them with alarmingly exotic animals, and on Sundays obliged his tenants to come to listen to the brass band which played in his 'Larmer Tree Grounds'. When excavating he would drive off on to the site in a high dogcart, accompanied by his carefully trained assistants, perched on penny-farthing bicycles, and displaying the General's colours round the brims of their boater hats. This man, who is personally so reminiscent of the eighteenth century, was, in fact, the immediate inspiration of the scientific archaeology of the twentieth. In the objectivity and detail of his excavation and the exhaustiveness of his publication he has never been outdone. His vast *Excavations on Cranborne Chase*, which appeared between 1887 and 1898, is in most respects a model of what such a publication should be when money is unlimited. In the private museum on his estate models were not only carved from solid mahogany, but were of meticulous accuracy. As a reward, his work can still be used to-day, often to support ideas of which he could have no conception.

The present century has seen another great change in prehistoric studies. Hitherto, as we have shown, it had not been the academic scholars who were interested in prehistory, nor yet the scientists, apart from its purely geological aspects, but the gentry, and then also the professional men, the parsons, lawyers, and doctors, whose affairs took them out of doors. But now more and more scholars, led by the Hellenists, began to concern themselves with barbarian archaeology, while, on the other hand, laboratory methods were utilized to make it more scientific. As the subject in this way grew increasingly wide and complex, it demanded to become a full-time study. While amateurs still make invaluable contributions to archaeology, its leaders are now professionals working at universities and museums. Probably past Fellows of the Society of Antiquaries would be shocked at the young men and women who sit on their red-leather benches to-day, people who use the study of antiquity as a means of earning their bread, and not as a cultivated pastime and opportunity for unrestrained speculation. But they would have to recognize that their achievements in recent years have been very great. Co-operation with classical scholarship is at last bridging the senseless gap which long divided Greek and Roman from prehistoric studies, so that we begin to get a unified picture of the classical and barbarian peoples who shared Europe and who impinged upon one another so often. Simultaneously the introduction of ingenious analytical techniques of the laboratory makes it reasonable for archaeology to claim to be in many respects an exact science.

Happily the result of all this has not been to make the subject increasingly academic and difficult. On the contrary, it has made it possible to get much nearer to early man, to see him as an individual, as a member of society, to divine something of his ways of thought and his emotions. It has been the main object of this small book to give some hints of this achievement to a wider public.

Bibliography

The list is for the most part limited to books published in the last twenty years. Simpler and more inexpensive books are marked★.

GENERAL

Prehistory and Civilization:

★V. GORDON CHILDE, *Man Makes Himself*. London: Watts, 1936. (Thinker's Library), 1939.

★V. GORDON CHILDE, *What Happened in History*. (Pelican Books, A 108.) Harmondsworth: Penguin Books, 1942.

★GRAHAME CLARK (J. G. D.), *Archæology and Society*, 3rd edition, London: Methuen, 1947.

EUROPE

C. S. COON, *The Races of Europe*. New York: Macmillan, 1939.

C. F. C. HAWKES, *The Prehistoric Foundations of Europe: to the Mycenean Age*. London: Methuen, 1940.

GEOFFREY BIBBY, *Testimony of the Spade*. Collins, 1957.

Palaeolithic:

★M. C. BURKITT, *The Old Stone Age*. Cambridge University Press, 1933.

I. G. D. CLARK, *Prehistoric Europe: the Economic Basis*. Methuen, 1952.

K. P. OAKLEY, *Man the Toolmaker*. British Museum of Natural History, 2nd edn., 1952.

Mesolithic:

J. G. D. CLARK, *The Mesolithic Settlement of Northern Europe*. Cambridge University Press, 1936.

Mesolithic to Bronze Age:

V. GORDON CHILDE, *The Dawn of European Civilization* (4th edn.). London: Kegan Paul, 1947.

BRITAIN
(mainly Mesolithic onwards)

*V. GORDON CHILDE, *Prehistoric Communities of the British Isles*. London and Edinburgh: Chambers, 1940.
  At present the standard work: contains full earlier bibliography.

*SIR CYRIL FOX, *The Personality of Britain: its Influence on Inhabitant and Invader in Prehistoric and Early Historic Times* (4th edn., 1943).

L. V. GRINSELL, *The Ancient Burial Mounds of England*. Methuen, 2nd edn., 1953.

*JACQUETTA AND CHRISTOPHER HAWKES, *Prehistoric Britain* (an extended version of the present work). London: Chatto and Windus, 1947.

*JACQUETTA HAWKES, *A Guide to the Prehistoric and Roman Monuments of England and Wales*. London: Chatto and Windus, 1951.

*JACQUETTA HAWKES, *Early Britain*. Collins, 1944.

BRUCE MITFORD, Editor, *Recent Archæological Excavations in Britain*. Routledge, 1956.

*STUART PIGGOTT, *British Prehistory*. Oxford University Press, 1949.

STUART PIGGOTT, *Neolithic Cultures of the British Isles*. Cambridge University Press, 1954.

England:
  *GRAHAME CLARK (J. G. D.) *Prehistoric England*. London: Batsford, 1940.

Wales:
  *W. F. GRIMES, *The Prehistory of Wales*. Cardiff: National Museum of Wales, 1951.

Scotland:
  V. GORDON CHILDE, *The Prehistory of Scotland*. London: Kegan Paul, 1935.

  *V. GORDON CHILDE, *Prehistoric Scotland*. (Historical Association Pamphlets, no. 115). London: Bell, 1940.

  *V. GORDON CHILDE, *Scotland before the Scots*. London: Methuen, 1945.

Special Counties:

*W. J. VARLEY AND J. WILFRID JACKSON, *Prehistoric Cheshire.* (Handbook to the History of Cheshire, no. 1.) Chester: Cheshire Rural Community Council, 1940.

*M. E. CUNNINGTON, *An Introduction to the Archæology of Wiltshire* (3rd edn.). Devizes: Woodward, 1934.

*E. CECIL CURWEN, *The Archæology of Sussex.* (County Archæologies Series.) London: Methuen, 1937.

*Other volumes in the County Archaeologies Series (London: Methuen) are:

H. J. E. PEAKE, *The Archæology of Berkshire*, 1930.

H. O'NEILL HENCKEN, *The Archæology of Cornwall and Scilly*, 1932.

R. F. JESSUP, *The Archæology of Kent*, 1930.

C. E. VULLIAMY, *The Archæology of Middlesex and London*, 1930.

DINA P. DOBSON, *The Archæology of Somerset*, 1931.

F. AND H. W. ELGEE, *The Archæology of Yorkshire*, 1932.

Special Sites (including some books earlier than 1933):

R. BRUCE-MITFORD (ed.), *Recent Archæological Excavations in Britain.* Routledge, 1956.

*A. BULLEID, *The Lake-Villages of Somerset.* (Somerset Folk Series, no. 16.) London: Folk Press (2nd edition), 1948.

R. J. C. ATKINSON, *Stonehenge*, Hamish Hamilton, 1956.

A. HAMILTON, *Jarlshof*, H.M.S.O., 1956.

Reports of the Research Committee of the Society of Antiquaries:

R. E. M. AND T. V. WHEELER, *Verulamium: a Belgic and two Roman Cities.* Oxford University Press (London: Milford), 1936.

R. E. M. WHEELER, *Maiden Castle.* Oxford University Press (London: Cumberlege), 1943.

C. F. C. HAWKES AND M. R. HULL, *Camulodunum.* Oxford University Press (London: Cumberlege), 1947.

Later Iron Age: Roman Britain:

Art:

   E. THURLOW LEEDS, *Celtic Ornament (to* A.D. 700). Oxford:
   Clarendon Press, 1933.

General:

   *R. G. COLLINGWOOD, *Roman Britain* (latest edn.). Oxford:
   Clarendon Press, 1934.

   R. G. COLLINGWOOD AND J. N. L. MYRES, *Roman Britain and
   the English Settlements.* (The Oxford History of England, Vol. 1:
   2nd edn.) Oxford: Clarendon Press, 1936.

   *IAN RICHMOND, *Roman Britain* (Britain in Pictures Series).
   London: Collins, 1947.

   *IAN RICHMOND, *Roman Britain.* Penguin Books, 1955.

Illustrated Regional Guides to Ancient Monuments, H. M. Office of
Works:

   *Vol. I, *Northern England*
   *Vol. II, *Southern England*   London: H.M. Stationery Office,
   *Vol. III, *E. Anglia and Midlands*   1935–9.
   *Vol. IV, *South Wales.*

Field Archæology, Maps, and Air-Photography (including some publications earlier than 1933):

   R. J. C. ATKINSON, *Field Archæology,* London-Methuen, 1946.

Ordnance Survey publications: London, H.M. Stationery Office:
   Field Archæology (notes for beginners). 2nd edn., 1936.

Maps:

General Map of the major visible antiquities of Great Britain older
than A.D. 1066:

   Ancient Britain: (1) North Sheet, (2) South Sheet. Scale, 10 miles
   to inch. 1st edn., 1951.

Megalithic Survey (maps ¼ mile to inch, showing distribution of
long barrows, megaliths, dwelling-sites, flint-mines, with lists
and explanatory text), comprising:

   Map of Neolithic Wessex.

   Map of the Trent Basin.

   Map of South Wales.

Celtic Earthworks of Salisbury Plain (maps, 1 : 25,000, showing
Celtic fields, earthworks, and barrows: one so far published):

Old Sarum (map covering the district around). Revised edn.,
1937.

Period Map (with explanatory letterpress):

Roman Britain. 3rd edn., 1956.

Air-Photography (author, O. G. S. Crawford):

Air-Photography and Archæology. (Wessex district: illustrated
with air-photographs and maps), 2nd edn., 1928.

Air-Photography for Archæologists (the subject illustrated by
typical examples). 1929.

O. G. S. CRAWFORD AND A. KEILLER, *Wessex from the Air*. Oxford: Clarendon Press, 1928.

L. V. GRINSELL, *The Archæology of Wessex*. Methuen, 1958.

PERIODICALS

General quarterly review of archaeology, equally for the specialist
and the ordinary reader:

Antiquity, edited by Glyn Daniel and published by H. W. Edwards,
The Wharf, Newbury, Berks; appears regularly in March, June,
September, and December.

Journals published by Societies:

The Prehistoric Society:

Proceedings of the Prehistoric Society, edited by J. G. D. Clark
(University Museum of Archaeology and Ethnology, Downing
Street, Cambridge). Appears normally half-yearly.

Society for the Promotion of Roman Studies (50 Bedford Square,
London, WC1):

The Journal of Roman Studies. Contains, in addition to articles, a
full summary account of each year's excavations: may include
prehistoric (usually Iron Age) as well as Roman material; appears
normally half-yearly.

The following are concerned with archaeology of both prehistoric and later periods:

Society of Antiquaries (Burlington House, London, W1):

> *The Antiquaries Journal* (normally quarterly).

> *Archaeologia* (normally a large annual volume).

Royal Archaeological Institute (Lancaster House, London, SW1):

> *The Archaeological Journal* (normally half-yearly).

Wales: Cambrian Archaeological Association (Whitford, Holywell, Flints.):

> *Archæologia Cambrensis* (normally half-yearly).

Scotland: Society of Antiquaries of Scotland (Edinburgh):
> *Proceedings* of the Society (an annual volume).

Most English counties have an archaeological society normally publishing a journal annually (a few more often).

The Congress of Archaeological Societies (in union with the Society of Antiquaries: Burlington House, London, W1 (published a small annual *Report of the Research Committee* of the Congress, which gave a summary account of all discoveries made during the year, and a bibliography of all articles in periodicals, and principal books, published relating to Prehistoric, Roman, post-Roman, and Medieval archaeology, for the whole of the British Isles. This appeared to 1939 inclusive.

A similar publication, the *Archaeological Bulletin for the British Isles*, has now been undertaken by the Congress's successor, the Council for British Archaeology (c/o London University Institute of Archaeology, Inner Circle, Regent's Park, London, NW1): the first issue, covering 1940–46, appeared in 1949, and is being followed by annual issues for 1947 and each following year.

The Council has also published, in 1948, a handbook entitled *Archæology in Great Britain: Survey and Policy of Field Research* (Part I, to the Seventh Century A.D.).

Index

ABBEVILLIAN, 22, 23
Abernethy, 127
Acheulian, 22, 25
Agricola, 157
Agriculture, 40, 83, 92–3, 107–8, 119–20, 141
Albert, Prince Consort, 162
All Cannings Cross, 123
Alpine race, 101
Alps, 105, 124, 140
Amber, 88, 90, 124, 137
Anchor, 138
Arbor Low, 81–2
Archaeology, 159–65
Archery, 45, 62, 71, 89
Arminghall, 65
Arrowheads, 35, 37, 45, 48, 54, 62, 71, 89
Art, 57–8, 130–1, 137, 152–3
Aryan languages, 69
Atlantic sea route, 42, 55, 58–9, 83, 131, 139
Atrebates, 144–5
Aubrey holes, the, 77
Aubrey, J., 160
Augustus, 152
Aurignacian, 29
Avebury, 15, 43, 73, 74, 81, 92, 161
Axes, bronze, 85, 89, 95, 98, 104, 113
    copper, 58, 70
    flint, stone, 22–3, 24, 47–50, 58, 61, 70
    iron, 141
    and see battle-axes, hand-axes
Aylesford, 141
Azilian, 31, 35, 37

BARROWS, long, 52–5, 60
    round, 72, 86, 91, 128
Battersea, 130, 151
Battle-axes, Battle-axe folk, 69–71, 88, 113
Beads, 46, 88, 90, 99, 100, 137
Beakers, Beaker Folk, 65, 68, 73, 77, 82, 86, 87–8, 92, 154

Beech Bottom, 143
Belgae, 140, 142, 143–6, 147, 148, 150, 151, 154–5, 158
Bigbury, 142
Birdlip, 130, 150
bits, 130
Bleasdale, 99
Blenheim Park, 154
boars, see pigs
boats, canoes, 32, 42, 44, 47, 86–7, 104, 135, 138
bone-work, 29, 32, 35, 47, 99, 112, 121, 136
Boucher de Perthes, 163
Boudicca, 126
Bourton-on-the-Water, 154–5
Boyd Dawkins, 163
Bredon Hill, 133, 155
Brigantes, 148–9
Brittany, 16, 55, 70, 81, 94, 133, 138, 149
brochs, 155
bronze, 40, 68, 83, 88, 103, 112–13, 114, 115, 118–19, 126, 135–6, 141, 149, 153
Bronze Age, Early, 67 ff., 152
    Late, 101 ff.
brooches, 127, 141, 152
buckets, 110, 114, 122, 141
burials, Neolithic, 52–5, 60
    Megalithic, 72, 82
    Bronze Age, 52, 72–5, 86–7, 89–91, 98–9, 114
    Iron Age, 123, 128–9, 140–1, 146, 153
Bury Hill, 147
buttons, 71, 104

CAESAR, 138, 140, 141–2, 146, 151, 153, 157
Camden, 160
camps, Neolithic, 35
    (forts) Iron Age, 112, 127, 132–4, 142, 147–8, 155
Camulodunum, 152–3, 157

172